Praise for *Ending Addiction for Good*

"If your world has been ripped apart by addiction, this book is a must read for you. The highly personalized, whole-health treatment protocol as described in these pages is among the best available in the recovery field today. I was excited to learn about it and thrilled when I saw the results of it. As Richard Taite writes, 'There is no better way to end the day than to know that an addict has found a new way to live and thrive.'"

Mark Jaffe, MD
Psychiatrist and Faculty at USC's Keck School of Medicine

"If you have a loved one or a friend who is on the road to becoming your lost one due to an addiction, you will find the information in this book extremely helpful in helping them to find the road to recovery. Its wisdom and authenticity come from such a place of love and hope."

Candy Finnigan, BRI ll
Interventionist on A&E's INTERVENTION and Author of When
Enough Is Enough: A Comprehensive Guide to Successful Intervention

"*Ending Addiction for Good* addresses both the adult and the child-in-the-adult to break the cycle of harm to the next generation while healing old emotional wounds. I'm a pediatrician; I have seen addiction hurt COUNTLESS children and families. A mother or father is just not present and available to be a skilled loving parent until they deal with THEIR addiction."

Jay N. Gordon, MD, FAAP
Assistant Professor of Pediatrics, UCLA Medical School
Senior Fellow in Pediatric Nutrition, Memorial Sloan-
Kettering Institute

"*Ending Addiction for Good* brings forward an approach that provides hope, restoration, and healing to the addict. Its power is that it addresses the whole person and defines a clear path toward freedom and a true sense of self."

Dominique Robertson, MFT, PsyD

"As an addiction specialist, I champion the Stages of Change model for addiction recovery. It not only targets and treats the root causes of addiction, but provides recovering addicts with the tools to believe change is possible and to develop the skills to create a sober life without the need to return to addiction."

Robert Waldman, MD
Addiction Treatment Specialist and Medical Expert on the Treatment of
Drug Dependency

"Kudos to Richard Taite and Constance Scharff, PhD, for sharing this evidence-based path that allows freedom from addiction. I have seen the most debilitated addicts recover using this recovery program. It is utterly amazing to see the healing that occurs and the resulting transformation in lives."

Damon Raskin, MD
Internal and Addiction Medicine

"This integrative approach provides the path to restored meaning and heightened purpose in returning those suffering from addiction to their essential state."

Peter Amato, MA
Author of Soul Silence *and Founder of Inner Harmony Wellness*

"The comprehensive addiction recovery method in *Ending Addiction for Good* has saved the lives of people dear to my heart. For that I am eternally grateful, and for certain, they are too."

Nicholas Vrataric
Executive Director of the Clare Foundation

"In thirty-five years of working with addicts, helping them live rather than die, I have never seen a treatment protocol as effective as that offered by Cliffside Malibu. I am thrilled that this lifesaving protocol is being offered to the world through the book *Ending Addiction for Good*."

Beverly Iser
Life Coach

ENDING ADDICTION FOR GOOD

*The Groundbreaking,
Holistic, Evidence-Based Way
to Transform Your Life*

RICHARD TAITE AND
CONSTANCE SCHARFF, PHD

Ending Addiction for Good: The Groundbreaking, Holistic, Evidence-Based Way to Transform Your Life

Copyright © 2014 Richard Taite and Constance Scharff, PhD. All rights reserved. No part of this book may be reproduced or retransmitted in any form or by any means without the written permission of the publisher.

First edition published by Wheatmark® 2012.

Published by Wheatmark®
1760 East River Road, Suite 145
Tucson, Arizona 85718 USA
www.wheatmark.com

ISBN: 978-1-60494-858-5 (paperback)
ISBN: 978-1-60494-917-9 (ebook)
ISBN: 978-1-60494-996-4 (audiobook)
LCCN: 2012951107

rev201402

Contents

CONTENTS

CONTENTS

Acknowledgments

From Connie

Turning this manuscript in to the publisher on the four-teenth anniversary of my sobriety, I am struck by how much my life has changed since the age of twenty-two, when I first admitted to myself that I am an alcoholic and wanted a different life. Today, my world is filled with wonder. I cannot be more grateful.

I would like to thank all those who made this book possible, starting with Dr. James Prochaska and his colleagues. His work has always been foundational to my understanding of how addicts recover. All addicts are in debt to his research. Without it, many would needlessly die.

I'd like to thank my coauthor, Richard Taite. I was honored that Rich noticed my addiction scholarship and asked me to be part of his team. We need voices like Rich's—voices sharing that recovery is for every addict. His encour-agement helped me persevere on this project even when I was less than convinced that it would come together.

Finally, I'd like to thank all the people who have sup-ported me through the writing process. I thank my excep-tional rabbi, Neil Blumofe, who absolutely refuses to let me dwell on the negative. I am grateful to Catherine Madera and

Debra Winegarten, two talented authors, who are support-ive of me on those days when writing is not the dream job I thought it would be. I'd also like to thank Neil Gumenick, Will Morris, Ellen Evans, Cindy Pettit Zieve, Chaya Rittger, Meg and Leigh Allen-Armistead, and Delphine Robertson for being tirelessly loyal friends. I receive so much love from my inner circle that it is difficult to imagine my life without them.

From Rich

This book project has been a dream of mine many years in the making. I am grateful to have found the right team to put it together.

First, I would like to thank Constance Scharff, PhD, for agreeing to write this book with me. She is a longtime friend of the family who I knew did "something" with addiction. When my wife explained Connie's views on addiction and that she had done extensive research on the Stages of Change model, I nearly fell off my chair. I am grateful for her dili-gence and patience with me.

I would like to thank Dr. James Prochaska and his col-leagues, students, and research assistants for their work on the Stages of Change model. Without this development in the field of psychology, I certainly would not be sober today, nor would I be able to help other addicts recover; I would be another casualty of addiction. Instead, I am blessed with the opportunity to help people transform their lives every day using the Stages of Change model. Dr. Prochaska's work, to me, is almost miraculous.

ACKNOWLEDGMENTS

My colleague, John Kenyon, is the professional who consistently pushes me to reach my potential and design the life I have always dreamed of living. John has taught me how to be a man of whom both my wife and children can be proud. I continue to value his advice and appreciate his service.

I would like to express a special debt of gratitude to the staff members of the Cliffside Malibu Treatment Center. It is through their dedicated service and commitment to helping every addict who comes through our doors that the treatment protocol in this book was built. I could not have completed this project without their insights, experience, and encouragement.

I also could not have gotten this project off the ground without my wife, Delphine Robertson, my assistant, Christa Volk, and the team's fabulous editor, Allison McCabe, each of whom in her own way gave me the tools and time needed to complete this book. They worked tirelessly, day and night, to help me meet the tightest of production deadlines; their efforts did not go unnoticed.

Finally, I would like to thank the addicts I have known throughout the years, from the clients at Cliffside Malibu to friends who have recovered and those who have not. I am especially indebted to those whose stories are shared in these pages. It is stories like theirs and the struggles of addicts seeking to recover that have made me grateful for my own recovery and inspired me to do the work that I do. There is no better way to end the day than to know that an addict has found a new way to live and thrive. To all of you who are fighting to overcome addiction, thank you for your courage. Believe me, a transformed life can be yours.

A Note from
Dr. James Prochaska

What a joy to be part of the journey of the many individuals who are helped through the stages of change at the Cliffside Malibu Treatment Center. I especially love how interventions at Cliffside Malibu begin by loving individuals into treatment. Through the personal experience of those helped by the treatment protocol in this book and by our science that was taught to us by one thousand ordinary people struggling to get free from their addictions you, too, can have hope that you can be helped wherever you are. Whether you are ready, getting ready, or not ready to take action, professional and personalized treatment helps individuals progress through the stages of change. Such progress can free individuals not only from the disorder produced by addiction; it can also free them to fulfill multiple domains of well-being. What a joy to be part of the journey of individuals transcending their suffering and their struggling to be in that special place of thriving.

—James O. Prochaska, PhD
Director of the Cancer Prevention Research Center
at the University of Rhode Island and developer of the
Transtheoretical Model of Behavior Change
One of the "Top Five Most Cited Authors in Psychology"
according to the American Psychology Society
Recipient of an Innovator's Award from the
Robert Wood Johnson Foundation

Foreword

When Richard Taite, a trusted colleague, asked me to read *Ending Addiction for Good* and write a foreword, I immediately agreed. In my psychotherapy practice in Santa Monica, California, I work with people with longstanding addictions who have been through treatment programs many times, but who have been unable to stay sober. I use the therapeutic methods that are described and explained in this book to help my clients, so I was understandably excited to see how the book had come out. I can say without reservation that the results have been successful. Richard and his coauthor, Constance Scharff, have written a book that deals with the complexity of the subject of addiction in a way that is readable and accessible. *Ending Addiction for Good* will help addicts and their families understand the problem of addiction so that they can create positive change in their lives.

Though addicts need holistic treatment in the first months or years of sobriety, psychotherapy that helps an addict or alcoholic understand the forces that cause him to abuse substances is critical to creating a foundation for his recovery. At Cliffside Malibu many different therapeutic tools are utilized to help addicts recover, but a focus on psychotherapy is at the heart of the program. I credit this focus with their success.

Not everyone agrees with this focus on psychotherapy. Some people are resistant to the use of psychotherapy for recovery from drug addiction because they believe that addicts will be encouraged to see themselves as victims and blame their parents for their problems. People often say, "Why look at the past? It's the present that's the problem." It is true that we can't change the past. But problems don't magically appear out of thin air; they develop over time. Today, the addict is struggling with a drug or alcohol problem, but his addiction is rooted in some earlier experience. Through reviewing the past in therapy, people uncover parts of their personal history they were only partly aware of at the time. Reviewing the past is not a way to blame your parents for your problems, reinforce your sense of victimization in the world, or avoid your own responsibility for solving your problems. Psychotherapy is a way to remember what happened to you and to consider the impact of the events in your life that you may have minimized or ignored so that you can move forward in the present in positive ways.

There are many factors that can cause addiction. When we are young, we are incredibly dependent on the caregivers around us to take care of our needs. If our caregivers are overly taxed or troubled during our early years or if they are struggling with anxiety, depression, marital conflict, health or financial problems, or perhaps their own addictions, these stressors make it difficult for even the most loving parent to meet the tremendous needs of a small child. This kind of neglect often results in the child searching for something to make himself feel better. The young child may escape into sports or imaginary games; this search for an escape is what may later lead the person to find a solution in drugs or alcohol.

We may also have problems finding ways to handle our

uniqueness. Determining our strengths and mitigating the weaknesses of our temperament are not always easy or obvious processes. It can be a challenge to find the better version of ourselves when we don't easily fit into the circumstances of our childhood environment. How does the young person cope with an early environment for which he is not well-suited? Some people struggle with tremendous shyness and begin drinking and using drugs to overcome social anxiety. Some people with learning challenges, dyslexia, or attention problems have added difficulties at home and in school and find they can function more effectively with the help of drugs or alcohol.

Addiction develops as a maladaptive tool we use to soothe ourselves, particularly when better options are unavailable. The world is frequently challenging, but as adults we are capable of defending ourselves, of adapting to stressors, and of finding ways to meet our needs. In childhood we are not well-equipped to defend ourselves. We are vulnerable to our environment and dependent on our caregivers to provide shelter, food, care, consistency, and all the love and attention that small children need. In searching through the events that happened in our childhood, we are not trying to find who is to blame for our pain, but rather to discover what happened to us, how we felt about it, and how it impacted us over time. In what ways were we injured? In what ways were our needs unmet? In what ways did we miss out on things like safety, support, reassurance, encouragement, direction, and hope when we really needed them?

People do not choose addiction, but rather, much to their surprise, find themselves trapped in it. The addict suffers from the illusion that he is making the choice to drink or use drugs, but he is not. He has lost the ability to face his pain without the addiction. Addiction is about pain. People suffering from addiction are not trying to destroy themselves; they are trying to survive yet another day. Survival has become their highest goal. They no longer believe that they can face the struggles of the world without the temporary pain relief that their addiction provides. They try with great effort to deny the damage that their addiction has caused to themselves, their lives, and the lives of their loved ones. They do not want to cause or live with the damage, but their lives are no longer under their control.

The program at Cliffside Malibu is set up to love people into recovery and to give them the tools and support they need in order to find their way back to a life filled with hope and happiness. This program's focus on holistic well-being using proven, evidence-based interventions is the best available. I have seen the results of focused psychotherapy in my work and Richard's in the form of happy, productive lives put to good purpose, in families restored, and in hope for the future where there had been none. I encourage you to read this book with an open mind and look for the ways in which you, your family, or your clients can benefit from a different kind of life.

—John Kenyon, PsyD

Authors' Note

This book presents information about drug addiction and alcoholism. It gives an overview of some of the treatment methods used at the Cliffside Malibu Addiction Treatment Center in Malibu, California, and discusses the understandings of addiction recovery that are present in academic and scientific research on the subject. Many people have found a new life using these recovery methods. However, there are many medical issues that the long-term use of drugs and alcohol can cause in an individual. Before you begin this or any treatment protocol on your own, we encourage you to see a medical doctor to determine how you can best be physically and emotionally supported through your drug or alcohol detox. Whether at our center or elsewhere, we want everyone who needs help to receive a supported, safe, and comfortable detox under the care and supervision of his personal physician.

Additionally, throughout the book we refer to the addict as "he." While addiction certainly affects men and women in equal numbers, we use the masculine pronoun for ease of reading. We found that using gender neutral language made reading the book cumbersome. We apologize if this troubles any readers.

In this book you will read the stories of addicts in recovery. While Richard's and Connie's stories are true-life accounts of struggles with addiction, the other stories in the book are composites of individuals who have recovered using the addiction treatment protocol outlined in this book. Composite stories combine the real-life experience of two or more people as well as fictionalized elements. We use composite stories in this book so that there is absolutely no way any of the addicts who have recovered at the Cliffside Malibu Treatment Center can be identified. It is of the utmost importance to us that the anonymity of those who are undergoing or who have completed treatment be safeguarded.

1

Richard's Story

My name is Richard Taite. I am the founder of the Cliff-side Malibu Addiction Treatment Center in Malibu, California. If you had told me twenty years ago that I would one day get sober, marry an amazing woman who consistently inspires me to be a better man, have two children who are the loves of my life, and become the founder of one of the leading addiction treatment centers in the world, I would have laughed in your face. Then I would have taken another hit of crack. I spent twenty years as a full-blown drug addict. For the first ten years, I never thought of stopping. Getting high was my sole purpose in life and was the most fun I had ever had. But for the second ten years of my addiction, I was trying and failing to get sober. I had ruined so much of my life by that time that I was demoralized and hopeless. I knew that I had to stop getting high if I ever wanted to have a normal life. But I couldn't stop. I had tried twelve-step programs and, even though I got a lot out of them, I needed more. Eventually, I found a solution.

If you have picked up this book, chances are that you fit into one of the following three categories: (1) you are struggling with a drug or alcohol problem and you are looking for help; (2) someone you love has a drug or alcohol problem and you want to know what you can do to help him recover; (3) you are in the addiction recovery field and interested in finding out more about Cliffside Malibu's unique treatment protocol. If you fit into these categories or simply want to know more about what addiction is and how it's overcome, you've got the right book.

I am not a writer, so I asked Dr. Constance Scharff, a PhD in Transformative Studies, to coauthor this book with me. Dr. Scharff is a longtime family friend who has been in recovery from alcoholism nearly fifteen years. She began drinking from the age of eleven to deal with longstanding physical and sexual abuse. By age eighteen, she was a full-blown alcoholic, and by twenty-two, drank two liters or more of hard liquor a day. After getting sober, Dr. Scharff went to graduate school to become an addiction researcher. She focused her attention on understanding the unfolding processes of change as they pertain to addiction. I was surprised and pleased to discover that much of her work is based on the research of Dr. James Prochaska, one of the world's foremost experts on change and the man whose psychological model formed the basis for my own recovery and the treatment we implement at Cliffside Malibu.

Dr. Prochaska's Stages of Change model helped me get sober. Since his work literally saved my life, I called to thank him and let him know how his model has revolutionized treatment for the addicts seeking recovery here at Cliffside Malibu. I was so filled with gratitude that I became emotional during the phone call. Because of my personal connection to Dr. Prochaska's work and the life it has given me, I was thrilled when he offered to endorse this book.

According to Prochaska's model, the process of behavioral change is similar for everyone. This process takes place regardless of which specific clinical tools are most appropriate to help each individual. When we use the Stages of Change process to facilitate an addict's necessary progression toward his recovery, we are helping him to create the foundation for a new and fulfilling drug- or alcohol-free life.

Treatment for addiction is constantly evolving as we determine what works to get and keep people sober. We have an evidence-base, a clearly defined set of practices that are proven to help people get sober. We have used the evidence-base to create a highly successful, unique treatment protocol. We have found that by combining a particular set of holistic, integrative interventions to help the addict on the levels of mind, body, and spirit, recovery happens with relative ease.

I know these methods work because without them, I was unable to stop smoking crack no matter how hard I tried. I was horribly sick and dishonest and no one wanted to help me. In my years of operating Cliffside Malibu, I have seen only a handful of addicts who were as bad as I was. Once I started working with a therapist whose psychological interventions were based on moving me through the stages of change, I was able to stop using drugs.

I was sixteen the first time I smoked crack. I dropped off my car to be serviced at a local repair shop and one of the mechanics drove me home. When we got to my house, he asked if he could use my bathroom. He was in there for a long time. After about twenty minutes, I knocked on the door to make sure he was okay. He came out sweaty and disheveled. He was holding a glass pipe with what looked like little white pebbles in it. When he asked if I wanted a hit, I didn't hesitate. I had been getting high daily since I first smoked pot with my best friend at age twelve. I loved the escape from reality and the euphoria pot gave me. When I was high, my awkwardness disappeared and I felt comfortable in my own skin. I put the pipe to my mouth and inhaled. The chemical hit my brain and the effect was strong and immediate. I felt incredible. I had snorted cocaine before and liked it, but this took the experience to a whole new level. It was the best feeling I had ever had in my life and I knew that this was the way I wanted to feel all the time. I was hooked. I did not draw a single sober breath for the next sixteen years.

At eighteen, I had my first arrest. I had just bought a gram of cocaine and was racing home at eighty miles per hour through residential neighborhoods because I was so excited to get home and smoke it. I blew through a stop sign, and the police pulled me over. They took me directly to jail.

I was just a kid and I had no idea what was going to happen to me. In the station, the cops had me sit on a wooden bench and handcuffed me to a metal bar attached to the bench. The guys sitting next to me looked like real criminals, and I was scared. I had the fold of coke in my underwear, and I was sure they were going to strip-search me and find it. I didn't know what to do, so I asked if I could use the bathroom, hoping I could figure out a way to get rid of the drugs. An officer uncuffed me and took me to a urinal. There was a cop next to the urinal above a low partition. As I undid my pants, I took the fold out of my underwear and emptied the powder into the urinal behind the partition. Then I dropped the paper fold into the urinal and peed on it. The officer cuffed me again and took me to a cell. My mother picked me up two hours later. I was not embarrassed or ashamed that I had been arrested. I wasn't even relieved that they hadn't found the drugs. I was annoyed that I had flushed a gram of coke for no reason. It never occurred to me that I had dodged a bullet; I didn't connect my enthusiasm for smoking cocaine with getting arrested. As soon as I got home, I got into my car and went to meet the dealer again.

It took me seven years at two institutions to get a four-year degree. In that time, I decided I wanted to be a lawyer. I got accepted to a bottom of the barrel law school that I don't think was even accredited at the time. At this point, my habit was so out of control that I couldn't make it through my first year of law school.

Before I knew that I had failed out of school, however, I realized that I was supposed to be interning at a law firm during the summer. I called an old friend of my dad's who got me a ten-dollar-an-hour job with an attorney. I started working for the attorney and got really good at it. I would settle cases and make a lot of money for him and the firm. When I started that job, my boss was driving a ten-year-old Honda and living in a two-bedroom apartment. Within a few months, he had bought a huge house in Encino overlooking the valley and was driving a new top-of-the-line Mercedes Benz. He quickly increased my salary!

But after six months, the owner of the firm fired me. My cocaine use was out of control. I was manic, loud, unprofessional, and unreliable, and I wouldn't show up for days at a time. My behavior was so unacceptable that even though I helped make the attorney a fortune and he knew that it would take four guys working full time to match my productivity, he didn't want me around. I wasn't worth the trouble.

A few months later, I began working with another lawyer and helped her to start her firm. My drug use continued to increase. At my new office, I kept a comforter and pillow in a filing cabinet. I would stay at that office around the clock, working during the day and smoking crack at my desk all night. At sunrise, I would get out the pillow and comforter and force myself to sleep for a couple of hours. I would be woken by the phone ringing at the start of the work day before people got to the office. I did this for years. Within three years, I was smoking every single night at the firm. My entire life had been reduced to getting high. Everything I did was for the sole purpose of acquiring and smoking cocaine. I never thought about living my life any other way.

One night in January of 1994, I decided to go back to my apartment. I had run out of money and felt like I needed one normal night of sleep to recover physically. That night the Northridge earthquake hit. It was one of the worst earthquakes in California history, and the Santa Monica promenade, where my office was, was devastated. My building was immediately red-tagged as uninhabitable. The morning after the quake, I sneaked through the tape in order to see my office. The brick wall behind my desk had collapsed, and my chair and desk were completely buried under bricks. If I had stayed at my desk that night smoking crack, as I usually did, I would have been crushed to death or buried alive.

Most people who find themselves in this kind of situation—barely escaping death—feel grateful or lucky. They resolve to live life more fully or think they were given a second chance because they have some purpose to fulfill. Not me. I remember thinking "We have to move our office," and then, "I need to get high."

My life continued on this downward spiral for years. Then I met Trish and Angela, two other crack addicts. Soon the three of us were inseparable. These two women taught me how to smoke crack "the right way." I was an amateur up until I met them. It had never occurred to me that you could smoke for more than twenty-four hours in a row. The healthy part of me, the small part that was still there, believed that you had to sleep every day. Trish and Angela showed me that I could smoke for a week straight with no sleep. The routine was: smoke cocaine, eat a Big Mac or some ramen once a week just to keep myself alive, pass out for twelve to fifteen hours and repeat. I once went thirteen nights without sleeping. This was my life and I loved it.

Trish, Angela, and I got high like this for the next two years. But after about three months, we started having problems. Sometime between the third and fourth day of getting high, Angela would always have a cocaine seizure, almost bite her tongue completely off, and bang her head on something, giving herself a concussion. The first time I saw this happen, I was horrified. I immediately came down from my high because I was so scared and shaken. But after the third or fourth seizure, I was desensitized. It was just another part of the weekly routine.

Then Trish got addicted to heroin and would shoot it and pass out. She would be asleep while Angela and I were smoking crack. One day she shot up so much that her breath slowed almost to a stop and she turned purple. I couldn't call for help because I hadn't paid my phone bill and the phone had been shut off. I was really scared and didn't know what to do. I realized she was dying, so I started blowing crack cocaine into her mouth, holding her nose closed and smacking her repeatedly. Then I threw her in a cold shower. After about a half hour of this, she woke up.

I was terrified that day, panicking and trying to figure out what to do to keep Trish alive. The first thought I had the next morning was, "I am so grateful that Trish didn't die." My second thought was, "Where's the pipe?" Trish's overdose was just a little interruption to our routine. We were incapable of choosing another way of life. Trish kept shooting up and Angela and I kept smoking crack.

Eventually, the money ran out. I hadn't paid my rent in so long that the landlord put a "three day notice to pay or quit" sign on my door. If I didn't pay my rent within three days, the sheriffs would be there to make sure I moved out. Once again, smoking crack was my priority. I threw the notice away and kept what money I had to buy more coke. When the sheriffs arrived, I left without taking anything. I had spent the intervening three days like every other day: smoking crack or figuring out how to get more crack. I had become homeless.

After abandoning that apartment and what was left of my possessions, I started living in what were basically "crack motels," places that charged around forty dollars a night for a bug-infested, dirty room with unwashed sheets in the worst neighborhoods in Hollywood, Los Angeles, and Venice. Everyone in those motels was smoking crack or involved in some other illegal activity and was looking for the easiest way to get money. I spent my days and nights paranoid; I didn't trust anyone. I knew the cops were watching my every move. When I couldn't afford even a crack motel, I snuck onto a friend's boat in the marina.

I knew I had to stop. I called Kevin, the one last friend I had who would not hang up on me. I told him I had been on drugs for years and that I couldn't do it anymore. I was homeless with no money or food. I started to cry. Kevin was my last hope. He always saw the good in me, even when I was convinced it was no longer there. He was disappointed that I had let drugs ruin my life, but he still cared enough about me to take me to the bank and get a cashier's check made out to a sober living house. That day I filled up my tank with gas, bought a carton of cigarettes and some beef jerky, and went into the sober living house. I started to go to therapy and made a commitment to myself to stick with it.

I needed to be in therapy for a long time in order to heal the old injuries that were keeping me self-medicating. Part of my recovery came through discovering the lies I believed about myself and replacing them with the truth. One of the major lies was "I am a bad person." As a child, I was told that I was bad, and I believed it. That old belief stuck with me and affected every part of my life. When my therapist uncovered that belief, he told me that it wasn't true, but I didn't believe him. "How old were you when you started feeling this way?" he asked. I told him I had always been bad, but I remember feeling it strongly at four or five. He became aggravated. "You were not bad!" he said. Then he asked me to imagine having a four-year-old son of my own. "Could that child be bad? Are any four-year-olds bad?" He made me aware that I had been carrying these beliefs from childhood into my adult life, and they were controlling my actions. He was frustrated because he saw how these old lies were blocking me from becoming who I was really meant to be.

There were many strongly rooted lies that had stuck with me since childhood, undermining everything positive in my life. Through therapy, I was able to realize that those lies were old injuries that have nothing to do with who I am today. I was able to let go of them. Without those old beliefs infecting my mind, I no longer wanted to crawl back under the covers and hide from the world. I no longer continued to damage my relationships and the world around me, sabotaging the successes and happiness in my life. I started to wake up excited about each new day.

As I got clean, I became aware of what worked for me and what did not. I began to think about my experience and wonder how these lessons could be used to help others. I began to read the sobriety research and speak to leading addiction recovery professionals. I found that a clear evidence-base exists, indicating exactly which types of addiction recovery tools are the most effective. I knew I could not effectively help addicts on my own, so I pulled together some of the leading medical and psychological professionals in the industry. I brought in top-notch alternative and complementary medicine practitioners. They helped me understand the addiction research. As a team, we combined and refined diverse therapies and created what would become the Cliffside Malibu treatment protocol.

I decided that my dream home would be the perfect setting for the kind of recovery center I envisioned. I had moved to Malibu at this point, to a beautiful white Connecticut-style farmhouse with one hundred eighty degrees of white water ocean views. I walked through the rooms of this house every day, thinking about how far I had come. Several years earlier I had been arrested for making a crack deal; now I was looking out at Catalina Island from my living room. I couldn't believe that a guy like me could have something so nice. I was peaceful there. It was my oasis away from the insanity of the city and the streets that still reminded me of my old way of life. Cliffside Malibu Addiction Treatment Center was born.

I had struggled so many times before to recover. I now believe that it was my dedication to my therapeutic process that made sobriety possible. I had made progress in therapy, but it was slow and incremental. I quickly realized, however, that if I'd had the resources and time available to be in therapy every day in a contained, safe environment, the process that had taken years for me could have been completed in a much shorter time. I began to think about how that process could happen for other people. Though it took me ten years of relapse and torment to get sober, our residents are able to recover in thirty to one hundred twenty days.

Cliffside Malibu staff members are the finest you'll find anywhere. They are attentive to the client's needs whether it's daytime or the middle of the night. I insist on my staff members being compassionate, empathetic, and aware. I will not hire anyone who has become desensitized to the process of helping people. If one of my clients wakes in the middle of the night scared or disoriented, someone will be there to be supportive while he processes his feelings and to explain to him what is going on. Our professional treatment team is also qualified to treat those with co-occurring disorders—people who have psychological conditions in addition to addiction. We do this because we recognize that many alcoholics and addicts have a variety of conditions that exacerbate their addictions.

In this book, you will find information about the scientific evidence behind addiction treatment. You will learn about the Stages of Change theory created by James Prochaska and his colleagues. You will learn what these experts have taught us about how addicts change by being engaged at the psychological level of readiness to change. You will learn about biological therapies, such as orthomolecular medicine and acupuncture that we use to heal the body so that the mind can then also recover. You will learn about neuroscience and how our new ways of understanding how the brain works are changing the way we view and treat addiction. You will also learn about the spiritual aspect of addiction and how to find a spiritual or meditative practice that works for you in your life.

The concepts discussed in this book are tried and true addiction recovery treatments. On their own, each has only a limited effect on the addict's ability to recover. Acupuncture or talk therapy or spiritual counseling will not get an addict sober when used independently. However, when these elements are woven together, not randomly but progressively and on an individualized basis according to the addict's needs, the individual seeking recovery is exposed to what he needs at the precise time he needs it. It is the synergy created by the application of the "right" treatments for the individual that creates the power needed for addiction recovery.

How do I know this therapeutic protocol works? In addition to the evidence-base, my staff and I see the results of these methods every day. Not every client receives every treatment; each receives the particular treatments he needs. Our method has been so effective that we have been able to guarantee our treatment. I believe, at the time of the printing of this book, that we are the only addiction treatment center to offer such a guarantee. For full information on our recovery guarantee, you can go to our website, www.CliffsideMalibu. com, and read the details of our guarantee program.

For a long time, drugs were more important to me than anything else, and I couldn't live without them. But I was hollow and rotten inside, and had no joy or love in my life. Today, I have the kind of life I never could have imagined for myself. The strength of the love I feel for my wife and children is overwhelming, more intense than anything I've ever known. I never knew I was capable of feeling anything this genuine.

I feel more alive and present when I'm with my family than at any other time. My addiction almost deprived me of this experience. I founded Cliffside Malibu because I know firsthand that recovery from addiction is possible. Because of my recovery, I am able to live my dreams. I help those who suffer turn their lives around and lead healthy, productive lives. I love knowing that people at my center leave having had a life-changing experience and that they are going to thrive from this point forward. These are the lives they were always meant to live before drugs and alcohol derailed them. This book offers the same path of freedom to you.

2

Connie's Story

I was born to Jewish pig farmers in California's Central Valley. My mother and father, raised in Los Angeles, had always wanted the country life. To help them, my father's parents purchased a twenty-acre ranch outside Fowler, California, where my parents had a peach orchard, a raisin vineyard, and a small pork operation of around thirty breeding animals. This was my first home.

The ranch could have been a magical place if I'd had a different family, but I did not have a different family. My mother was an angry woman, ill-prepared for the difficulties and isolation of farm life. When I was no more than five or six, she would lock me and my little brother out of the house for the whole day. I'd knock on the door to complain that we were hungry or thirsty, to which I would get the response, "Drink out of the hose." Famished, I would climb the fruit trees trying to find one or two pieces of fruit that were ripe. I'd be beaten if my brother or I ate any of the grapes because those were a commercial crop, but I could pick a peach or two without being detected. If I found an edible fruit, I'd throw it down to my brother. The best time of year to be locked out was after the peaches were ripe and picked. Late ripening fruit would fall to the ground, and my brother and I could eat our fill. At least we weren't hungry those days. To this day, I still hate eating peaches because it reminds me of that time.

My father was a thousand times worse than my mother. When I turned seven, while my mother was away with my brother picking up a cake for my birthday party, my father raped me for the first time. It was the beginning of three years of sexual abuse and torture. I have very little memory of those years. Mercifully, the brain protects us as best it can from that level of trauma. What I do remember was feeling incredibly small. How much does a seven-year-old weigh? Perhaps fifty pounds? My father was three hundred pounds or more. The memory of feeling the crushing weight of him and fighting to breathe against his bulk, even through my late thirties, woke me screaming in the night. It wasn't until I was thirty-seven that I could celebrate my birthday without tears.

Against this background of abuse and neglect, it is little wonder that I started drinking. I remember my first drink well. I was eleven years old. My parents had divorced, and I had gone with my mother to live in Oregon. On this particular afternoon, she and my brother were away in town. I had just finished my chores in the barn. I came into the house—a decaying, single-wide trailer—walked over to the cabinet where my mother kept the liquor, and poured myself a full glass of booze using a shot or so from every bottle. I had no mixer. I couldn't take much from any one bottle because my mother very rarely drank and she'd know in an instant if the bottles had more than a small amount removed. Then, I stood over the sink and drank it down. The concoction tasted terrible! But I wasn't drinking for the taste. Innately, I knew that the liquor would lessen my pain. I don't know where the knowledge came from; it was just there. When I'd finished the whole glass, I rinsed it out, returned to the barn, and lay on the hay bales to enjoy the feeling of being high. I drank to get drunk every opportunity I had after that.

In the country, it was difficult to get my hands on alcohol. Oregon sold liquor in state-run liquor stores that had limited hours. I lived so far out of town that being in town when the stores were open was a challenge. I still managed to get drunk now and again. However, everything changed for me when I got to college. In college, there were plenty of people who would buy for me until I was old enough to buy for myself. I spent a lot of time drunk. I showed up for classes drunk. I took finals drunk. I got alcohol poisoning and puked in the sink in my dorm room. I blacked out. I passed out. I tried to smoke pot a few times, but I hallucinated terribly so I went back to drinking.

At the end of the first term of my freshman year, I had a near-breakdown. I developed wonderful friendships in college with people who are still my friends today. I didn't know how to leave them and go home to face my family over the winter break. I had never been treated as well by my family as I was by my friends in college. I didn't want to go home. Besides all that, I had no access to alcohol at my mother's house.

I was so distressed about going home that I took only thirty minutes to complete a three-hour final exam. After the test, one of my friends pulled me from bed and took me to the counseling center where I lay almost catatonic on the therapist's couch while he spoke to her about my home problems. Their consensus was that since I was no longer in danger of being raped or beaten, I had to go home for the break. The therapist gave me her home phone number and told me to call her if I had any trouble while I was away.

When I returned from winter break, I began to see that

therapist. I knew I had no chance of resolving my drinking problem unless the pain of childhood incest, physical abuse, and neglect were confronted head on. Unfortunately, I was so traumatized and dissociative that much of the time I found myself unable to speak. I often found that I'd spend my entire session sitting on the therapist's couch, shaking, never saying much more than a word. When the session was over, I'd go immediately back to my room, about a one-minute walk from the counseling center, and drink. I wasn't then able to face my past, but I kept trying and drinking and trying again.

Though sheer intelligence carried me through college and I graduated with loads of honors, I knew that I was dying. I didn't expect to live beyond twenty-five. I hadn't realized that the purpose of college is to prepare a person for a job, and so I flitted from one temporary position to another. There was no point in building a career if I knew I was going to die. I spent some time in the UK and then in New England, working and drinking. I had no money and no plan.

That's when the miracle happened; ten months after I graduated from college, my father died unexpectedly of a heart attack. I had an opportunity to live.

Though I truly wish no one ill, including my father, I see my father's death as a blessing. I could not recover while he was alive. I couldn't push against him while he was alive. I couldn't talk about what he did to me when he was alive. I couldn't help but feel sickened every time I saw him, even though he stopped abusing me just before my parents divorced and we moved away. But with him gone, the reality of my alcoholism became apparent. I saw clearly that I wasn't drinking "at" or "because" of him anymore. If he was my problem, I should have been able to stop drinking when he died, but I could not stop drinking. I knew then that I was an alcoholic; I was twenty-two years old.

I asked for help from Andrew, a colleague who was sober. He had a great deal of patience with me. The only way I could talk about my alcoholism was to get really drunk. I'd tell him that I wanted to stop drinking, but I didn't know how. The next morning, I would have only vague recollections of our conversation and would be embarrassed by my drinking, but Andrew didn't seem to mind. He said that alcoholics get drunk and that I shouldn't worry about that just then. All I had to do was want to recover and try a little bit of controlled drinking to be sure that I had a problem. The experiment was a miserable failure. I was absolutely certain that I was an alcoholic and could not stop drinking on my own.

When Andrew and I both ended up living in Southern California three or four months after our temp job together ended, he took me to a few twelve-step meetings and helped me meet some good women who would look out for me. Although I was undiagnosed, I had post-traumatic stress disorder (PTSD) so bad that I found it almost impossible to go anywhere without Andrew when I wasn't high. I was terrified and trembled if anyone got near me. I hit someone once who tapped me on the shoulder from behind. It was suggested that I go to women's groups so that I would be less scared. That helped a little bit with my fear, but not much. I did my best to do what I was told and I spent more time sober than drunk in my first three years trying to get sober, but I still relapsed several times before finally getting sober in 1998.

While I liked the twelve-step model because I am naturally a spiritual person, I found that I needed help the program could not give. Most of my problems were not caused by my own shortcomings. I didn't ask my father to rape me or my mother to beat and neglect me, yet those were the issues that most often caused my drinking. As the symptoms of my PTSD worsened in my sobriety, my friends and I knew that I would soon relapse if I did not find additional support to give me the psychological help I needed. A very good therapist was suggested to me, and I began to see her regularly.

As before, I was so traumatized that I could not verbalize what I wanted to say. For much of the first year that I saw my therapist, I would have to write little notes to her before our sessions to let her know what I wanted to talk about. We'd do exercises in which I'd just try to say the word *incest*—to which I would respond by opening my mouth and sputtering. There I was, a woman in my mid-twenties, smart as a whip, and accomplished in college and my work life, but I couldn't say one short word. I felt hopeless and ashamed. Later, when I could speak, the things I had to say were so difficult that I would immediately dissociate and find my consciousness floating above the room. Talking about the experiences of my past was almost as traumatic as living through them. But I kept going back because I believed that not only would this work help me maintain my sobriety, but would also help me to have the life about which I dreamed. My father had taken so much from me. I wanted to get some of it back.

I want to be clear that even in those difficult times, I still experienced sobriety as a miraculous gift. I was a two-liter-of-hard-liquor-a-day drinker when my father died. At twenty-two years old, my organs hurt. Some of them, like my liver and kidneys, were distended. I was hung over all the time.

Most of all, I was tired. I was so very tired. But, sober, my life was incredible! My body did not hurt and I had energy to do things. I also had money. The fifty percent or so of my income that had gone to drinking could now be freely spent on other things, like food or going to the movies. More than all that, though, I had hope. I was alive and my father was not. I thought I'd be dead by twenty-five. I intended to make something of myself, no matter how difficult my recovery might be.

My sober friends gave me the courage I needed to face my past. Even though I was a grown woman, I still felt, and in some ways acted, like a little girl. I was always hiding. I knew my father was dead, but that little girl part of me was sure that something would happen, and he would come back to hurt me again. I didn't know how to be vulnerable with anyone. My defenses were nearly impenetrable. Yet, people really seemed to like me. I never had trouble making friends anywhere I went. Those friends were steadfast and patient. They watched me struggle, and it hurt them to see me as a generous, kind, and loving person who was so deeply hurt that she couldn't always share what she really wanted to. I would tease that they should wait until I got better because I'd hug them so tight that their stuffing would come out and likely never let them go.

The hardest concept for me to come to terms with was that my father was a despicable man. I would try to believe, through various mental contortions and re-imaginings of my history, that my father was somehow not the awful, abusive man that he was. I wanted both him and my mother to be proud of me. I wanted them to care. Eventually, I had to accept that my father was what he was and that my mother gave me the best she had to offer and cared about me in the only way she was able. None of this was my fault. It was just the luck of the draw. My job, if I wanted to remain sober, was to repair the old wounds and not worry about anyone else. Eventually, I went to graduate school. Initially, I earned a master's degree in leadership to enhance my opportunities in nonprofit management, the field I worked in during much of my early sobriety. I didn't have the confidence to follow my dreams. What I really wanted to do was study addiction and learn how, after our bodies recover from addiction, our minds and spirits also grow and develop. I wanted to know why, if addiction is a disease, we needed spiritual work to make our lives better. The truth was that I was already working with other addicts and helping them as best I could to find a path to recovery. I was especially drawn to the people in recovery who struggled with the same kinds of issues I did. Many of these were war veterans returning from Iraq and Afghanistan. I shared my experience with them and we helped one another, but we all had the same trouble staying sober. It is nearly impossible to stay straight when the almost unbelievable horrors of your past come rushing in without notice. I knew that those who suffered as I had needed better tools to improve the quality of their sobriety.

After my master's, I was immediately accepted into a PhD program at the California Institute of Integral Studies in the field of Transformative Studies. Transformative Studies is the study of change in all its forms: biological, psychological, spiritual, organizational, and interpersonal. After first studying general ideas about change, I wanted to apply what I learned in general to addiction in particular. I wanted to know what psychology, neuroscience, medicine, philosophy, and religion had to say about addiction recovery, one of the most complete forms of change a person can go through. What can be done to help addicts in early and long-term sobriety stay sober? I also wanted to know what could be done for people like me, people who had debilitating experiences that made their chances of getting and staying sober less than average. I knew there had to be help for us; I believed this with all my heart. I became an addiction researcher so that those who have the most need to drink can recover too.

What do I do as an addiction researcher? I look at all research that can be applied to addiction recovery to see if it is scientifically sound and safe. There is some incredible research being undertaken in the fields of medicine, psychology, genetics, and neurobiology. However, much of this research has not been applied to addiction recovery. I bring this research to the attention of the clinical staff at Cliffside Malibu so that we can offer it to our clients. Additionally, I speak at major international conferences worldwide on these findings, to make what we learn available to all those involved in both research and addiction treatment. My passion is to make addiction recovery as painless and effective as possible. Addiction was once a problem for which there was little hope for a solution. This is no longer true.

My world blossomed, personally and professionally, as I dove into addiction research. One of my colleagues in my doctoral program was William Morris, a world-renowned acupuncturist. He shared with me resources about acupuncture and holistic medicine. I started to receive acupuncture and found it to be the missing link in my recovery. Suddenly, my mind, body, and spirit were all being attended to. Acupuncture not only grounded me but also gave me a new strength and courage to move forward in therapy. I could talk about my past without being overwhelmed by it. Acupuncture also made me want to exercise, and I began to work out regularly with a trainer. I began to feel less ruled by my past and more hopeful about my future. Sobriety became easy; it was no longer something I worked for, but simply the way I lived my life. It was no more difficult than breathing. The thought of relapse became horrifying. Even when life presents its challenges, I do not ever consider picking up a drink.

While I researched for my dissertation, I found the work of Drs. Prochaska, Norcross, and DiClemente. As I read about the Stages of Change model and the transtheoretical approach to psychotherapy, I understood why I had needed a holistic—mind, body, and spirit—approach to recovery. Recovery wasn't only about abstaining from drinking. Given my past, simply abstaining from alcohol was a nightmare. Liquor kept the memories at bay and allowed me some functionality, though limited, in the world. Being sober without spiritual, psychological, and physical support was difficult beyond imagining because my past spilled into the present. Before acupuncture, for example, as many as forty times a day, I had body memories of being raped by my father. It was nearly impossible to stay sober against such experiences, but I did. I kept telling myself that the miracle would come.

True recovery, living a peaceful and happy life, is about overcoming the difficulties of our pasts. I needed a strong focus on mental health and overcoming fear in order to be sober and happy. I needed to learn to live in the hope of and in action toward what I wanted, not in fear of a man who was long gone. As I dove into my dissertation, I learned more and more about how psychology, biology, and spirit are linked together in intricate and almost indiscernible ways. This is true for the addict and non-addict alike. I also realized that recovering from addiction did not have to be as difficult for others as it had been for me. If given the proper tools, recovery can be achieved and maintained in ways that just happen and allow sober living to become one's natural way of life.

I don't want to give the impression that my world is all sunshine and roses. I am certainly a work in progress and have areas in which I can improve. For example, my father hated fat women and, so, to this day, I still feel more comfortable carrying a significant amount of excess weight. I realize that there are health implications for my size, but I remain at ease with my present weight for now. Because of the traumas in my past, I have not found it easy to date and, though I'd very much like to, I have not yet had the opportunity to marry. I also recently had a surgery that will prevent me from having children. The medical problem that caused the surgery to be necessary was likely caused, at least in part, by the severe sexual abuse I endured at so young an age. Loss of the ability to have children has been devastating, but I will grow from it.

Yet, even with these challenges, I still do not think of drinking. I have an incredible life. I have traveled the world, visiting amazing locations in Asia, Africa, and North America. I have also met with healers of all types to learn their wisdom as it can apply to addiction recovery. I have developed a strong commitment to my faith and have been graced with an encouraging rabbi who has the gift of being able to make me laugh even in the most challenging of circumstances. I have fantastic friends. At the time of my surgery they rallied around me, taking care of me, cooking the most incredible meals, shopping for me, doing my laundry, and just sitting with me. I moved to a town I enjoy and bought the house of my dreams. It's a showcase for all the treasures I've brought back from my travels. I write for a living. In addition to writing about addiction recovery, I also write poetry and prose. I am an authority on addiction recovery and help people every single day to choose to live a good life. I am even blessed to work with an outstanding charity in Kenya, helping children from one of the world's largest slums gain access to education in an effort to lift them out of the most extreme forms of poverty. I never imagined any of this could be mine, but it all is.

I should be dead now. People with histories like mine usually kill themselves outright or die the terrible deaths that addicts often experience. But I am alive, sober, and thriving. I won and my father lost. I have the opportunity not only to live my life, but to share with others the secret to getting and staying sober. I get to save lives—the lives of good people who suffer. Who in their right mind would turn down a second chance like that, even on a bad day?

3

The Nature of Addiction

If you had seen either of us when we were using, you would not have recognized us. You would not have guessed that one would become the founder and CEO of a cutting-edge addiction treatment center and the other a PhD in Transformative Studies who is a leading expert in maintaining long-term sobriety. Yet each of us was able to get and stay sober using the exact principles outlined in this book. We are an addict and an alcoholic who, year after year, have led sober, productive lives.

The same thing can happen for you or the one you love. To put you on that path of recovery, we will first help you to understand what addiction is. By learning this, you'll later be able to learn why and how addicts recover.

What is addiction? Can addiction be cured? Is there one main cause of addiction? Is one kind of treatment better than another? If I was once an addict, will I always be an addict? These are questions that you have probably asked yourself and others. This chapter will examine those questions and provide answers.

Alcoholism and Drug Addiction Defined

When we think of alcoholism or drug addiction—terms that will be used synonymously in this book—we think of a person who abuses a substance to the point that it causes consistent problems in his life. For example, a person who is addicted to alcohol will show up drunk to his daughter's wedding or regularly drive while intoxicated. The addict cannot stop himself from engaging in the problem behavior, in this case drinking, even though it is creating social and physical turmoil for him. He has lost all choice in the matter. He must drink despite the consequences. Most of us would identify a person who behaved in this way for an extended period of time as an addict.

In the clinical world of addiction treatment, defining addiction is more complicated than the example given above. Addiction and substance abuse are currently most widely defined using a psychomedical syndrome model. This means that addiction is defined by a variety of behaviors along a continuum. People must exhibit a particular set of characteristics to be diagnosed as addicts. These symptoms include: abnormal, often excessive patterns of alcohol and/ or drug consumption; increased tolerance to the substances used; withdrawal symptoms when the substance is removed; and, sometimes, serious health issues related to drug abuse. Addicts persist in using their drug of choice despite efforts to change their behavior or negative consequences resulting from their behavior. They also show an inability to predict how much they will use on a particular outing or to moderate the amount of a substance they consume. Eventually, using takes over all facets of the addict's life. The idea of addiction is often associated with the term "dependency." These terms are used synonymously.

Addiction is different from substance abuse. Substance abuse is simply the misuse of alcohol or other drugs. We might consider a night of binge drinking on New Year's Eve to be alcohol abuse. Using sedatives other than as prescribed for a short period following the death of a loved one is drug abuse. However, in order to cross the line to drug addiction, the abuse must be consistent, and the individual must begin to display the symptoms listed in the paragraph above. Drug and alcohol abuse is common, but it may or may not be the start of an addictive process.

What Is the Nature of Addiction?

There are many different ways to describe addiction. The three most common descriptions are as a moral failing, a disease, or a behavioral disorder. Throughout history, addiction has been seen as a moral failing; people become addicts because they lack good values. Today, addiction is usually classified as a disease; people become addicts because they have a genetic predisposition to use substances inappropriately to deal with life's problems. Others see addiction as a behavioral disorder; people become addicts because they engage in behaviors that eventually become habituated and unresponsive to conscious control. This lack of control leads to profoundly problematic consequences. Each of these ways of viewing addiction may overlap with the others.

The question addicts and their loved ones are really asking when they want to know about the nature of addiction is, "How did we get here? How did I become an addict?" These are good questions. It is important to understand where addiction comes from before trying to define it.

Addicts have a very specific set of traits. All addicts engage in behaviors that ease anxiety and reduce pain. The problem is that these behaviors become excessive and the consequences life-shattering. The teen who feels largely ignored by his parents finds that using cocaine makes him feel good about himself. The parent who is stressed out from having two children under the age of three finds that taking a few extra prescription anti-anxiety pills makes her day easier. The college student who is terrified to tell his parents he's gay finds that club drugs lessen his fears and improve his sex life. The office manager who throws out his back finds that the pain medication he is prescribed also reduces his stress levels. The sexually abused woman finds that drinking before sex lowers her inhibitions and makes the interaction possible. Initially, in all of these cases, the use of the substance seems to give the person, who is not yet an addict, relief from some sort of pain or anxiety. At least at first, drugs seem to make life easier.

Eventually, the using behavior escalates. Because the initial source of pain has not been dealt with, the moment the effects of the substance wear off, the pain returns. The person must use again. In an attempt to keep the pain under control, he becomes more and more entrenched in a pattern of dependency on the substance that becomes more important than anything else. At this point, the person has become an addict; he has lost the power of choice. He returns to his addictive behavior because he must. He does not want to forget his child's first communion or drive his car into a ditch; those consequences are the natural effects of his inability to stop covering his pain with behaviors that do not address the root causes of his suffering. Tragically, the addict adds the shame and embarrassment of the consequences of his addiction to the initial pain he was dealing with in the first place. This is the addictive process that shatters lives.

Addiction is rooted in an individual engaging in a behavior that gives him relief from pain. Addicts eventually find that they cannot stop engaging in these behaviors without aid. In time, the negative consequences of engaging in the addiction damage the addict's life on all levels: physical, mental, and spiritual. Finally, the addict ends up dead or wishing that he was. To varying degrees, these characteristics are found in every addict.

Knowing now the nature of addiction, we should review the main definitions of addiction because how addiction is defined and understood from a clinical perspective will make a great deal of difference in how addiction is treated.

Addiction As a Moral Deficiency

Excessive drinking and drug use has probably existed since man first learned to make wine or chewed the leaves of plants that gave him a rush. Almost from the beginning, those who overindulged were viewed by society as moral degenerates or weak-willed people. They frequently became social outcasts. These drug users were judged harshly because they seemed to "choose" to use the drug rather than attend to family or work obligations. The view of alcoholism and drug addiction as a moral failing was rarely challenged until the twentieth century.

Aversion therapies are commonly used to treat addiction when one believes it is a moral failing. The Romans made alcoholics drink from glasses with spiders in them. Addicts in China would be shot if they did not recover within a year of going to rehab. In some places, electric shock therapy and chemical aversions are still used to treat addiction. All these therapies are based on the assumption that addicts have a choice about their using and, if properly prompted, will make better choices.

At Cliffside Malibu, we patently reject the idea that addiction is a moral failing. Addicts use because they have a biological need (physical addiction), a strong set of ingrained behaviors, and an inappropriate relationship with their drug of choice (psychological addiction). In order to consider addiction a moral issue, a person must demonstrate that the addict has enough control over his behavior to be able to make a clear choice between one action and another. This is not the case. Even though the addict loves his family, he becomes so caught up in his addiction that he is compelled to use drugs or drink even when the consequences to his relationship with his family are catastrophic. There is no situation in which he can keep himself from using, for he will get high no matter the consequences. He may injure someone while driving drunk. He may commit infidelities. He may act out in rage when he is in a blackout and remember none of the harm he caused. He may lose his job due to substance abuse. None of this will cause him to stop using for any appreciable period. The addict engages in using even though he doesn't want to, even though his life and the lives of others are being destroyed. There is no element of choice once addiction has taken hold. The addict uses because he must, regardless of the consequences.

We do not use any aversion therapies at Cliffside Malibu primarily because they do not work. There is nothing in the evidence-base to suggest that shock therapy or chemical aversion treatments have any efficacy at all in treating the underlying causes of addiction.

Addiction Defined As a Disease

The most popular view of addiction in the United States today is based on the disease model. This model is not new. George Washington's Surgeon General originally introduced the disease model in the late 1700s, though it was not widely accepted until much later. In colonial America, addicts were flogged, not hospitalized. It wasn't until World War II, when medical screenings identified large numbers of alcoholics, that the disease model of addiction began to flourish.

Elvin Jellinek, of the Yale Center for Alcohol Studies, clearly defined the disease model of alcoholism in his book *The Disease Concept of Alcoholism.* According to Jellinek, the addictive process is a progressive and potentially terminal condition requiring lifelong abstinence as the best means of treatment. He describes the condition as a biomedical syndrome characterized by an inability to control or abstain from using, an increased tolerance to the substance used, and withdrawal symptoms when the substance is discontinued. Since Jellinek's initial definition of the syndrome, the disease model has expanded to include a genetic predisposition to addiction that is triggered by trauma and the misuse or abuse of addictive substances. Though addiction is considered a multilayered problem with both psychological and spiritual components, the disease model roots addiction firmly within the body, genetics, and biochemical processes of the mind.

The disease model of addiction is widely accepted in the medical community. The American Medical Association changed its view of alcoholism to the disease model in 1957. The World Health Association, the American College of Physicians, and the American Psychiatric Association have all followed suit. Even the *Diagnostic and Statistical Manual of Psychiatric Disorders*, commonly referred to as the DSM, uses a syndrome model to define drug abuse and drug dependency in a way that is similar in scope to Jellinek.

The DSM, a publication of the American Psychiatric Association, is used by psychologists, psychiatrists, and other health care professionals to diagnose mental health issues. It is issued by a medical association and used for medical billing. This in and of itself places addiction firmly within the purview of medicine, which largely understands the human condition through the lens of disease.

Classifying addiction as a disease has been beneficial in some ways. First and foremost, the disease model has created willingness to open treatment centers and rehabilitation facilities for addicts. At these treatment centers, a variety of recovery protocols have been tested. As these treatments are used and addicts do or do not recover, an evidence-base is built. When the research is published, more treatment centers are able to implement those practices that have the best results. In this way, the treatment of addicts is constantly evolving to be more and more effective. When we treat addicts, rather than shaming them, they have the opportunity to recover.

Cliffside Malibu is focused on recovery. Whether or not addiction is a disease is less important to us than the actual process of healing. We use the term disease in our facility and in our advertising because it is a concept with which people are comfortable and familiar. However, in our clinical programs, we use a different definition of addiction that we believe is more accurate and more descriptive of the work we do to help our clients make real and lasting changes. We use a behavioral model of addiction.

Beyond the Disease Model of Addiction

Though extremely popular, the disease model of addiction has its shortcomings. Detractors have noted that addicts are routinely absolved of crimes because of their "illness." Many people believe that pharmaceutical companies use the "disease" label to medicalize a social issue and take advantage of addicts looking for a magic pill that will cure addiction. Others contend that referring to addiction as a disease constitutes a form of social control; people who make unpopular lifestyle choices are urged to find treatment to change their ways. In other words, if I don't like the choices you make, the people you hang out with, or the way you live your life, I'll try to force you to conform to how I want you to live by making you go to treatment for your "disease."

Stanton Peele, a psychologist and addiction researcher, is perhaps the nation's most outspoken critic of the disease model. According to Peele, it is dishonest to suggest that addiction is a disease as it has no disease agent.

What does Peele mean when he says that addiction has no disease agent? Consider two examples: cancer and the flu. Cancer progresses through the growth of tumors. There is a clear biological process causing the illness. Tumors spread and damage the body until it can no longer function. We can test for cancer and find evidence of it in the body. The flu is a different type of disease, but a disease nonetheless. It proliferates through a virus. We can see the virus under a microscope and find evidence of it in the blood. In each of these cases, there is an obvious and tangible agent or pathogen causing the disease.

Alcoholism and drug addiction have no disease agent,

even if there are biophysical complications associated with the disorders. Your doctor can run tests to diagnose you with cancer or the flu, but there is no such test for addiction. He will not find any tumors, viruses, or other clearly defined signs of something causing disease. Addiction is more like dementia. It is classified as a "disease" by using a group of symptoms to define the disorder. A disease is a medical concept with a specific medical definition. We believe that disorder, rather than disease, is the more accurate term for addiction.

Alcoholism and drug addiction are behavioral problems that will eventually disrupt body systems, not the other way around. The addict becomes deeply entrenched in a pattern of behavior that includes the abuse of substances. Eventually, this using pattern becomes so much a part of the addict's life that his entire identity may be affected; he is unable to see himself as separate from the behavior. From this perspective, addiction is a classic example of a behavioral disorder.

What about the genetic component to addiction? The evidence so far is inconclusive. Geneticists are still working to delineate all the connections between addiction and genetics. Although the entire human genome has been mapped, the precise "addiction gene" or gene series remains elusive. There are at present at least three dozen genes that are believed to be associated with addiction, but the mechanism by which they create the opportunity for addiction to take root is not yet understood. While some studies suggest certain ethnicities show greater propensity to addiction, any unambiguous connection between the role of genetics and behavior has not yet been established. Observation tells us that addiction seems to run in families or is more prevalent in specific cultures, but we do not conclusively know why this is the case. There are potential causes other than or in addition to genetics that may play a role. Further, genetic mapping does not indicate who will become an addict; it can only show susceptibility to addiction. In layman's terms, unlike having genetic code for blue eyes that will cause you to manifest blue eyes, a genetic predisposition for addiction would have to be "turned on" by environment and behavior. Even if you have the genetics for an addict, you may not become one.

Even among the foremost experts in the field of addiction treatment, there is no consensus on how to define addiction in a way that is absolutely true. We acknowledge multiple perspectives on the subject and believe that no one is benefited by arguing about whether or not addiction is a disease. Instead, we help addicts change their lives so that using is no longer desirable. The focus of treatment is on using proven best practices to help addicts recover.

While addiction may not be clearly classified as a disease and the debate about the disease model could continue for decades, what we do know without a doubt is that addicts lead painful lives. This pain, not genetics, is what we see as the root of addictive behavior. Sometimes the pain starts with a traumatic event or series of events. Sometimes it is triggered by the neglect of our essential human needs for safety, support, and kindness during our formative years. In order to alleviate that pain and stress, the addict begins to drink or use drugs. Even if one accepts the idea of a genetic or biological vulnerability of any kind to addiction, there has to be something to trigger that vulnerability. Something has to tip the addict over the edge. That trigger is almost always trauma or profound neglect.

Since we consider alcoholism and drug addiction a behavioral disorder, rather than a disease, we have a broader treatment perspective than many other treatment centers. If addiction is a behavioral process, we know for certain that the addict can absolutely change behaviors and return to normal living. This isn't true with disease. Sometimes people recover from diseases and sometimes they don't. As addiction is a behavioral disorder, this means your loved one can fully and completely overcome addiction. That is our message of hope. Our clients go from having a dysfunctional set of behaviors to having a healthy set of behaviors. People change and recover to lead full, healthy lives.

Self-Sabotaging Behaviors and Self-Analysis As a Tool for Recovery

We choose to describe addiction as a disorder rather than a disease because we are interested in motivating people to change. What is it then, exactly, that motivates people to change from self-destructive patterns to positive ones?

Some people find comfort in the idea of understanding addiction as a disease. They can accept their addiction by saying, "I just have this disease; everyone has to struggle with something and this is my thing to struggle with." That's logical and understandable, but viewing addiction in this way denies the addict the opportunity to reflect on the events that happened in his life in order to analyze how they might have contributed to his addiction. If the addict says to himself, "I have a disease and I will never fully recover," he may not ever address the core issues of why he drank excessively or abused drugs. Consequently, addicts may find themselves slipping into old habits even after a considerable time abstaining from their drug of choice. In a way, the disease model of addiction can function as a psychological defense against looking at trauma.

Addicts and addiction professionals must look beyond the biological components of addiction to help people examine the difficult issues in their pasts that they have spent their lives avoiding. Addicts must examine and resolve these issues if they are going to recover. For us, it is less useful to know whether or not an addict has a set of genes that give him a propensity toward addiction than to know what specific set of events or feelings may have triggered the addictive behavior in the first place. We need this information so that we can help the addict understand and resolve his early traumatic experiences and regain control of his life.

Processing the traumatic events of our past is difficult and painful. The addict has developed his own coping mechanism to circumvent this pain using drugs or alcohol. The drug allows the addict to withdraw from reality and avoid his core issues. The drug's effects cover the pain of trauma. When the drug wears off, it must be ingested again. This process continues until drug use is so deeply ingrained that it is the main, habituated activity in the addict's life. Take away the drug and the pain of the original trauma comes barreling to the surface. To prevent this, addicts continue to participate in avoidance behaviors, even if they don't like them or know they are destructive. This self-defeating cycle is what addiction is really about.

When the addict is ready to set aside his self-sabotaging behaviors—whether they are using, cutting, over-exercising, sex, or anything else used to distract the addict from his core issues—he must learn to examine his life in a way that will help him to understand where his impulses come from. Then he must replace his familiar pattern of acting out with a different, healthier pattern of coping to cement his life change. With the help of a knowledgeable, trained, compassionate, and talented therapist, the addict can face the traumas of his past and learn the skills necessary to work through difficult events in the future. This set of skills is critical for sustained recovery.

The core issues of the addict's past must be addressed. Every addict begins abusing substances for a reason, whether conscious or not. No one picks up heroin or cocaine or any other drug for the first time and says to himself, "I'm going to take this until my teeth fall out, I lose my family, and die." Usually, the addict takes a small amount of a drug and notices that he feels better and is more able to cope with his life. Meanwhile, his subconscious is saying, "Hey, all that stuff that hurt a lot doesn't hurt anymore. But when the drug wears off, the pain comes back, so I'm going to take the drug again." Drug use is insidious; the repetition of the behavior begins slowly as a buffer against psychological or physical pain and increases as the addict discovers he needs to take the drug in greater and greater quantities in order to achieve the same effect. Eventually, the addict believes that he cannot live without drugs.

Why does the addict keep repeating the same behavior over and over again? He is searching for the good life. He is searching for happiness and release from suffering. Initially, the addict experiences the illusion of a happy, suffering-free life from the use of drugs. He confuses the momentary absence of pain with happiness or the good life. What the addict experiences is not the good life at all. Depending on circumstances, it is doubtful that the addict has ever experienced a good life. He likely doesn't know what a good life is. Drugs, because of the euphoria they create, make the addict believe, for a short time, that he is thriving. Certainly, not feeling the pain of old trauma is good. However, sobriety is better; it means being able to release the effects of the old pain for good. This is the foundation for a full and sustainably happy life.

Personalized psychotherapy is critical to the success of any addiction treatment program. After detox, when the difficult feelings from the past begin to surface, the addict needs a caring professional to help him work through those feelings. It doesn't matter what the difficult situations in the past were. Traumatic experiences include rape, child abuse, chronic neglect, an auto accident, combat-related trauma, the early loss of a family member or close friend, physical or emotional abandonment, adoption, or guilt over the addict's neglect of children or family. The extent and effect of the trauma is dependent on the individual and how he has learned to process and cope with it. The addict needs assistance processing his feelings, putting relationships right whenever possible, and developing new skills for living and for dealing with difficult situations in the future.

Difficult situations are not confined to the past. Challenging circumstances arise constantly. Children make mistakes and get into trouble. Conflict will arise between spouses. Parents grow older and may need more of our attention. Work will demand more of our time than we are able to give. We will face challenges, illnesses, accidents, financial difficulties, and all other manner of obstacles. That is the nature of human existence. Can you think of even one person who lives what we would consider a truly charmed life, with no conflict or difficulty at all? It's doubtful. Even in the best of times, trials exist and fortunes rise and fall. If he is provided with the right set of tools to ensure his lasting recovery, the addict will be equipped to meet even life's most difficult challenges.

The addict's work, if he is to remain sober long-term, is to learn how to face these challenges without using. At first, it can be difficult for the addict to brush his teeth or make his bed without needing chemical assistance. However, as time progresses and the addict learns new life skills through his work with a devoted therapist, overcoming life's small obstacles becomes easier. Eventually, all actions become easier. The addict's intensive psychotherapeutic work and willingness to develop self-analysis skills enable him to face even the most challenging hurdles with dignity and to maintain his recovery.

There Is No Cure for Alcoholism or Drug Addiction

There are addiction treatment programs that claim they can "cure" addiction. We do not believe that is true. No treatment center cures anyone of alcoholism or drug addiction. To suggest otherwise is to give the addict false hope for a magic cure. Addicts always look for magic cures. The promise of a cure fuels the addict's fantasy that everything can get better with the wave of a wand. There is an expression that addicts are like pickles; they can never become cucumbers again. Treatment can give an addict the skills to live a full, meaningful life, but it will never completely remove the addictive mindset from the individual. In that sense, there is no "cure" for addiction.

Addicts, however, do recover. We regularly see our clients thriving, living full and meaningful lives. Addicts who have achieved lasting recovery have a joy for living and are able to realize their full potential. These transformations occur because the addict has learned how to change his behavior. He becomes a vastly different person because he leads a vastly different life. Before entering treatment, an addict's day is filled with using, pushing back trauma, and lying to family and friends to enable his using to continue. After treatment, addicts spend their days engaged in useful work and meaningful, honest interactions with loved ones. They become fully present participants in their own lives. As days pass, the using pattern begins to lose its hold on the addict's thoughts and actions. Before too long, the addict begins to notice that it is easier not to use than it is to get high. After a period of time, the addict literally no longer thinks about using. This change is almost unbelievable for the addict.

In the first days or year of recovery, the addict is still in the using mindset; his new sober life is not yet fully habituated. Eventually, though, sobriety is so natural that the idea of using drugs feels like an impossibility. The addict's life has been transformed. That is the hope of recovery, not to be magically cured, but for the addict to find his true nature, realize his full potential, and change his habits so that his best self can thrive in his daily life.

The Value of the Cliffside Malibu Treatment Protocol

At Cliffside Malibu, we work from the assumption that addiction is a behavioral disorder with co-occurring physical, mental, and spiritual issues. We do not believe that the addict is a "bad" person (the moral failing model), nor do we accept that addiction is rooted first in the body (the disease model). We believe that addiction is rooted in the mind, in the habit-driven response to coping with pain. In other words, whether the addictive behavior started as a result of peer pressure, a longing for social acceptance, or a desire to obtain the euphoric effects substances give, by the time addiction has taken hold, the addict uses drugs and alcohol to avoid pain—physical, mental, and spiritual. Through intensive one-on-one psychotherapy and complementary treatments, we help the addict change his behavior and consequently change his life so that using is no longer necessary and it is no longer desired. The addict will prefer his sober life to his life of addiction. This transformation happens every day. It can happen for the addict you love too.

Addict in Recovery: Amy Green

When Amy Green's daughter said, "Mom, you're an addict and you need help," Amy called it "the most mortifying moment of my life." At fifty-six years old and with no family history of addiction, Amy simply couldn't believe that she had become an addict. But she knew that her family was right, that she needed help, and so she went to treatment without complaint.

Amy came from an affluent family in Vermont. She attended Wellesley College. While there, she met a rower from Harvard. They married quickly and had three children, two boys and a girl. Her husband, a tall, handsome man, took a job in sales that kept him traveling a great deal, but brought the family financial security. Amy didn't like that her husband was away, but she reveled in providing a wonderful home life for her children. She volunteered in their classrooms, was active with the PTA, served as a Cub Scout leader, and was a member of the choir at the family's church. In many ways, she thought of herself as a real life June Cleaver. Her children were healthy; her family was happy. Her husband was a solid provider, and he loved her. Life was in every way good.

A year after her youngest child left home, Amy's mother developed Alzheimer's. Watching her mother's slow decline was devastating. Amy and her husband agreed that they would move her mother and father in with them, demolishing a wall between two of the children's former bedrooms to create a second master suite in their house. As Amy's mother's mental state deteriorated, she began to share stories that Amy had never heard before. One day, Amy's mother began to recount the day that Amy was adopted, something Amy had never heard about. Confused, Amy confronted her father. Had her parents been lying to her all these years? Was she adopted? Amy's father said that they had never intended to tell Amy that she was adopted, but, yes, in fact, that was the case. Amy was stunned. She couldn't conceive of her parents as anything other than her biological parents, and she also couldn't understand why they would have lied to her about her parentage. She felt betrayed. When Amy's father offered her a small wooden box containing her adoption papers and baby photos, Amy accepted it with a mixture of disbelief and anger.

Amy learned that she was the daughter of her mother's youngest sister, who had drowned just three months after Amy was born. Amy's father, unable to deal with the grief of his loss, hanged himself after his wife's funeral. The family was devastated, and Amy's mother took in her niece as her own. The adoption was handled quietly and privately; no one ever spoke of Amy's biological mother again. As Amy sifted through newspaper clippings about her biological mother's accident, her heart broke. She was furious that she had learned about this so late, too late to have a complete and lucid conversation with her adoptive mother about what her biological mother had been like. An incredible sense of loss took hold of her—the loss of the mother she never knew, the loss of the mother she had loved her whole life, and the loss of her children who had moved away and were living their own lives. She didn't know how to even begin processing her feelings.

Then, one day while unloading groceries from her car, Amy slipped on a patch of ice and fell. Her back was damaged so much that she needed surgery to repair it. After her surgery, Amy was given prescription medication to ease her pain. A month after her operation, Amy's mother passed away. Still having difficulty walking, Amy collapsed into grief and depression. She asked her physician for an antidepressant, not telling him that she was still taking the pain medication prescribed by her surgeon.

Soon, Amy was mixing opioids and antidepressants with disastrous results. She was constantly nodding off and falling, often injuring herself. Her family had no idea how to address her behavior. Amy's husband gently tried to suggest that something was wrong, but he got nowhere. It frightened Amy's father to see his daughter in such a fragile state. He, too, tried to talk with her but to no avail. She refused to engage anyone on the subject. Her children were afraid to approach her, having seen their father's and grandfather's failed attempts. They were concerned that she would become alienated if she believed the family was ganging up on her. Meanwhile, Amy clung to the idea that she needed her medicine because her back ached and she was depressed over her mother's death and the secrets her parents had kept. It became very easy for her to justify her behavior to herself. Ironically, Amy didn't realize that she was now the one hurting her family. Amy simply could not see that she had a problem.

Eventually, after Amy was found unconscious and unresponsive in her yard and was taken to the hospital for a drug overdose, her children planned an intervention. This intervention was particularly heart wrenching, with her children, in-laws, husband, and father almost inconsolable and begging Amy to get help. As Amy came to see that she had a serious problem, she was overwhelmed with shame. She agreed to seek treatment only because she was assured that the treatment center was extremely protective of client privacy. She didn't want anyone to know how low she had fallen.

During the ninety days she was in treatment, Amy blossomed. She faced the feelings of abandonment and grief she felt over her children moving away and finding out so late in life that she had been adopted. She was introduced to acupuncture for pain management and yoga to improve her flexibility and release stress. She loved both treatments and continues them to this day while using only occasional, non-narcotic pain medication for her back. As her physical pain came under control and she learned to accept and understand her family's decisions, Amy's mood lifted. She no longer needed antidepressants. Amy now uses meditation to help her regulate her feelings. She has a sun room in which she sits in the morning after her breakfast, quietly finding the strength to face her day.

Amy's recovery was focused on finding a purpose for herself. She had always been someone's daughter or mother. Without those roles, she succumbed to prescription medication abuse because her pills, she freely admitted, made her pain go away. But Amy is no longer stuck in the past, numbing herself because of the difficulties of life. To fill her days, she became a part-time children's advocate and found that the challenges and joys of being around children again helped her feel useful. She also took up painting, something she had always wanted to do but hadn't had time for when her children were small.

Of her recovery, Amy says, "Every day is a joy. I wake up in a family that doesn't keep secrets anymore. My father and I talk over breakfast. My children come to visit often with the grandkids. We all laugh together. There is real love in my family. I would never have experienced this without recovery. The sober life is a blessed life."

4

The Cliffside Malibu Approach to Addiction Treatment

Integrated medical therapies consist of a combination of Western medical approaches and complementary or alternative medical practices. We also include in this term psychological treatment, spiritual development, and recreation (for balance). At our facility, doctors, psychotherapists, and nurses may assist clients with their personal needs. A client's psychiatrist or personal physician can prescribe medication if a client needs it. Medications are particularly helpful in easing discomfort associated with the detoxification process. We also have acupuncturists, massage therapists, yoga instructors, and other practitioners of complementary medicine who work with our clients. In a single day, a client might receive treatment from his own personal physician, an acupuncturist, and a massage therapist; have a session with a clinical therapist and a yoga instructor; and receive two visits from a nurse. This is how integrative medicine works.

Holistic medicine treats the whole person. It is based on the idea that the mind, body, and spirit are interconnected and cannot effectively be treated separately. This is especially true in addiction treatment. Alcohol and other substances affect every layer of an individual's life: his body, his mind, his emotions, his personality, his relationships, his perspective on life, his self-esteem, perhaps even his sense of his soul. Holistic addiction treatment methods recognize that we can't simply detox a person, get his body off drugs, and send him on his way expecting that he won't return to using. We must acknowledge, nurture, and heal the entire addict—mind, body, and spirit—so that he can become free of his addiction and experience a happy and fulfilling life.

Integrated and holistic therapies are combined to create our treatment protocol. Each addict needs to be supported in every way possible from the very first day of treatment. No matter what their area of expertise, our staff members work to improve all aspects of each client's well-being. For example, gourmet chefs work closely with our entire professional team to create delicious, well-balanced, and nutritious meals in order to help clients recover physically by regaining the strength and stamina that is needed to do the psychological and spiritual work that recovery requires. This synergistic approach to healing is the foundation of each addict's treatment.

Understanding the Effects of Substance Abuse on the Mind, Body, and Spirit

Mind

The addict's mind is different from the non-addict's mind. This is one of the main ways in which an addict can be differentiated from a non-addict. Have you ever been frustrated with an addict's behavior and asked yourself, "Why does he do that?" The simple answer is that he doesn't think the same way that you do and therefore doesn't act in the ways you expect him to.

To help you understand the way an addict thinks, ask yourself this question, "What motivates me in life?" Do you get out of bed for your children or your spouse? Do you love the work you do so much that even if you didn't need the money you earn, you'd still do the job for free? Those are not the kinds of things that motivate an addict. An addict in his addiction is motivated by the fear of pain. The addict knows that there will be emotional and physical pain to contend with if he stops using. He is unable or unwilling to face that pain, so he continues to use. He uses despite the needs of his spouse, his children, his family, his friends, his work, or his other obligations. He uses because everything in his being tells him that the pain will destroy him. He may not even be conscious of his motivations or aware that he is acting in this way at all, but it is pain that drives him.

Addicts use a substance again and again to avoid pain. This repeating pattern creates the habituated behavior that is addiction. Each time the addict uses, he is rewarded with a temporary reprieve from the pain of physical or emotional trauma. There might be additional benefits to his using; he may have a great time partying, have great sex, or find that his inhibitions are lessened and he is able to do things he is not able to do sober. The addict uses repeatedly because of the positive reinforcement he receives from these rewards. A habit is formed.

Though we help the addict at the levels of body and spirit, and believe that the addict cannot recover unless his health is addressed holistically, it is the area of the mind where addiction develops and it is here that we place our emphasis with psychotherapy.

The foundation of our psychotherapy programming is the Stages of Change model that was mentioned in Chapter One and will be explained in detail in Chapter Six. Using this model, we evaluate the client to determine which stage of understanding he is in when it comes to his addiction. Some people who come to treatment deny they have any problem with substance abuse at all. Others recognize their problem, are aware of their triggers, and have been working to make changes at home, but need the boost of treatment to make their efforts successful. At whichever stage of change the addict finds himself, we help him recognize his psychological processes so that he is self-aware and able to make healthier choices in the future. Using this model in our intensive psychotherapy progression allows us to help addicts break their addictive behaviors and lead healthier lives.

Body

The physical issues that develop with drug and alcohol addiction vary by the type of drug used, the frequency of use, the amount used, and the length of time the addict has been abusing the substance. Consider three examples: prescription medications, alcohol, and methamphetamine.

The three types of prescription medications most commonly abused are opioids: painkillers such as Vicodin, OxyContin, and Dilaudid; central nervous system depressants, such as barbiturates and benzodiazepines, which are commonly prescribed for anxiety, epilepsy, and insomnia (well-known brands include Nembutal, Valium, and Xanax); and stimulants for attention deficit hyperactivity disorder (ADHD) such as Ritalin and Adderall. People who abuse depressive substances, particularly those who mix opioids and benzodiazepines, are at risk for extreme drowsiness and injuries caused from sleepiness (e.g., falls, concussive injuries, automobile accidents) and depressed breathing. Brain function and respiration can become dangerously low, sometimes causing death. Other physical repercussions for prescription medication abuse, particularly stimulants, include anxiety, paranoia, dangerously high body temperatures, seizures, irregular heartbeat, heart attack, and stroke.

Alcoholics may develop liver, kidney, and pancreas problems. These problems can manifest as cirrhosis, cancer, or pancreatitis, among other diseases. Alcoholics who are predisposed to diabetes can become diabetic from ingesting the massive amounts of sugar found in alcohol. Excessive drinking can also cause injuries from falls or accidents due to lack of coordination and potentially fatal esophageal deterioration as a result of alcohol damaging the cells lining the esophagus. With prolonged abuse, brain damage can occur. These are only a few of the physical issues related to alcohol abuse.

Methamphetamines affect the body in a very different way. Superficially, meth ages the skin rapidly and can deteriorate teeth to the point of severe decay and loss known as "meth mouth." Smoking meth can cause sores around the mouth. Injecting meth can cause a number of infections that create lesions and, in some cases, lead to loss of limbs. Methamphetamine use causes elevated blood pressure and tachycardia (high heart rate). The elevated body temperature associated with meth use can permanently damage major organ systems. Meth use also erodes the brain, causing permanent brain damage with long-term use. As a result of meth's harmful effects to the body, users have a significantly increased risk of heart attack and stroke, both of which can cause permanent damage to body systems or death.

These three examples of the ways drugs affect the body, although very different, demonstrate how physically damaging addiction can be. Very few clients come to treatment in a good state of physical health. We use a client's detailed drug history to determine first how to help the client detox and, second, how to bring his damaged systems back to a state of balance. Our approach to returning the body to health is relatively simple: provide adequate time for rest and exercise, proper diet including nutritional support through ortho-molecular medicine and the use of organic foods whenever possible, and supportive Western and alternative therapies to strengthen the body. The healthier the body, the more available the mind is to do the concentrated psychological work necessary for a full recovery from addiction.

Spirit

The spirit is the most difficult aspect of a person to treat because what makes each individual's spirit thrive is deeply personal. However, there is no question that an addict's spirit is damaged by his using. We can all see it in the addict's face; it's as if the light has gone out behind his eyes. The spirit sickness of addiction manifests as a belief that life cannot improve, that there is no hope that addiction can be overcome at all, and certainly not for good.

Many addicts manifest what we call "learned helplessness." Learned helplessness is the state when the addict has given up—mentally, spiritually, and sometimes even physically—and believes there is no hope for change. Even when given the opportunity to take care of himself, such as through an offer to go to treatment, the addict will decline. He will not try to care for himself because he thinks he has no control over his situation. Believing that there is no way to overcome his addiction, the addict may resign himself to an addict's death. Learned helplessness is, above all, a spiritual depression.

The spirit's recovery can be addressed in several ways, thus allowing each client to discover and build upon what works best for him. We offer yoga, meditation, and nonreligious spiritual counseling. We encourage those with a connection to a particular faith tradition to rely on that. In addition, all clients are introduced to twelve-step programs.

Although ours is not a twelve-step based facility, we acknowledge that millions of people over the last seventy-plus years have found that twelve-step programs greatly assist them in their spiritual growth. These results are part of the evidence-base. People find companionship and support in twelve-step programs. Those who dedicate themselves to participating in twelve-step work find that they are able to maintain their sobriety for years, if not permanently. It would be negligent for any evidence-based treatment facility not to offer twelve-step programming to its clients. Some of our clients feel that twelve-step work is a positive experience. For those clients, we provide access to these meetings on a regular basis. Some of our clients have no interest in twelve-step programming and, after an introduction to what that path has to offer, choose to use different activities for their spiritual development.

No matter what is most comfortable to the addict, our professional team is flexible in working with the client's likes and dislikes. We assess his level of readiness to pursue an interest in spiritual work and then add that work into his therapeutic program as is most appropriate for his recovery.

The Importance of Personalized Treatment

In the Cliffside Malibu treatment protocol, all clinical programming revolves around individualizing every aspect of a client's day to meet his personal needs. No two addicts are alike and no two clinical treatment plans are alike.

Many clinical treatment programs using the disease model of addiction rely on a set schedule of predetermined therapeutic activities. If addiction is a disease, then all clients should respond similarly to the same treatment. For example, if you give insulin to a diabetic, you expect his blood sugar to drop. This is not true of addiction treatment. Even addicts with similar using histories will respond differently to the same treatment because of their different personal backgrounds. Because each individual addict differs so widely from his fellows and because we see addiction as primarily a behavioral disorder, we individualize all our treatment activities.

What can you expect from individualized treatment? First and foremost, each of our clients meets regularly with a deeply committed psychotherapist to help the addict understand the root causes of his addiction. The best way for an addict to develop the deep levels of trust required to do the work necessary to overcome addiction is to have one therapist dedicated to his recovery. This therapist will push and challenge him to face the life events and choices that habituated his using and created his addiction. The therapist also knows when not to push, when to allow time for contemplation, and how to provide nurturing support. This process of urging the client to examine his reasons for using, giving him tools to change his habits, and providing time to review the work done moves the addict through the stages of change, enabling him to end his addictive behaviors and lead a healthy life.

In our protocol, therapists are carefully selected to meet the needs of the individual client. During the first three to four days of treatment, while physicians are ensuring that the client's detox is as comfortable as possible, the clinical team is carefully observing the client to determine which therapist on the team would be the best fit. We have many therapists on hand, each with a different set of skills, training, and personal background. We believe that our staff dedicates more work, preparation, and attention to the client in the act of choosing a therapist and planning the initial stages of his treatment plan than most other centers provide in the entire first month of treatment. We do this because we recognize how critical finding the right fit with a therapist is to the success of the treatment plan.

Each client's psychotherapist oversees the individualization of his complete treatment plan by meeting with and/or reviewing records with the client's personal physician and psychiatrists, nutritionists, chefs, acupuncturists, equine therapists, massage therapists, personal trainers, yoga instructors, life coaches, clergy, and family members—literally everyone who will play a role in the client's recovery. The therapist, working with other professionals, coordinates every stage of the client's care, changing it when necessary as recovery becomes more deeply rooted. The therapist walks an ever-changing path, noting which therapies the client best responds to and strengthening areas of deficiency. We have found that this coordination of efforts provides clients with the most dynamic and effective treatment plan possible.

Can people overcome addiction and remain sober without individualized treatment? Yes. With dedication and commitment and often with a great deal of pain, relapse, and backsliding, people do get sober using treatment methods that are not personalized. However, individualized treatment that meets the addict at his level of personal readiness for change, that addresses his particular physical, mental, and spiritual needs, and that moves forward at the pace most appropriate for him will provide the addict with the time and space to embrace recovery and cement it as an integral and ordinary part of his life. While individualized treatment may not be the only way for an addict to achieve sustained sobriety, it is the most comfortable and effective.

The Value of Intensive Psychotherapy

When evaluating addiction treatment programs, it is extremely important to find out how often the client will receive personal, intensive psychotherapy. In some programs, the answer is never. There are treatment centers that do not offer individualized therapy and instead rely on group therapy sessions run by a sober addict or less-than-fully-certified counselor. While these programs are valuable, it is clear that a program that provides hours of personal therapy each week with a skilled professional is going to have superior results than getting to share your feelings for a few minutes in a group. We do not want to underestimate the importance of programs that are available to low-income and uninsured individuals. Almost any therapeutic setting will provide some assistance in helping an addict get sober, especially if he is motivated. However, intensive, individualized therapy has better results than other psychotherapeutic activities.

Intensive personal psychotherapy forces an addict to create a true bond with a trained, dedicated professional. The addict must develop trust and respect for boundaries in order for the therapeutic relationship to develop. The addict must learn to be honest and to share not only the truth about his using, but also about the events and circumstances about which he is most ashamed. The addict must learn to communicate and to describe his truest feelings. He must learn to take criticism and hear other viewpoints about life in general and his actions in particular. He must learn to accept encouragement and care if he is unaccustomed to those experiences. He must learn what his triggers are, why he used, why he wants to be sober, and how to make a plan to change his life.

With intensive psychotherapy, our attention is entirely on the addict's recovery. Clients respond to this individualized focus and are motivated to do the work to recover. The desire for recovery comes more easily and naturally when the addict meets regularly with someone who truly has his best interests at heart. Of all the benefits of intensive psychotherapy, that might be one of the best. The addict comes to believe that he is more than the totality of his mistakes and that he is in fact the vibrant, loving person he always hoped he could be.

Addict in Recovery: Neil Marchand

Neil Marchand is a national hero. Twenty-eight years old when he sought treatment, Neil was a Marine and recipient of the Silver Star for valor in the face of an enemy. He honorably served one tour in Iraq and two in Afghanistan and was wounded in action twice. The second time, Neil was disabled by a shrapnel wound that damaged nerves in his right leg. This caused him to require a cane if he was to walk any distance. Despite his injuries, this officer was polite, dignified, and honorable even at the height of his drug use.

Neil grew up in the country outside a small town in Texas. His was a traditional home. He said, "Yes, ma'am" and "Yes, sir" almost as soon as he was able to speak. Neil's father worked as a contractor and managed family oil investments. Neil's mother stayed home with her four children, three girls and Neil, the youngest. On his parents' thirty-five-acre ranch, all the children had chores, including taking care of the cattle and putting up hay. Every Sunday, the family went to church together. Sometimes, when Neil would nod off during the preacher's sermon, his father would reach over and smack him on the back of the head. Neil was not allowed to disrespect his elders or God. In every way, Neil's upbringing was "all-American."

Outside school, the ranch, and the church, Neil dabbled in rodeo, but wasn't serious enough about it to become a professional rodeo cowboy. What he really wanted, what he dreamed about, was to be a Marine and fight for his country.

Neil did not enlist in the military immediately after high school. Instead, because he wanted to become an officer, he matriculated at Texas A&M and joined their ROTC program. He was an exceptional student and cadet. After graduation and further military training, Neil became a commissioned officer with the U.S. Marine Corps.

Neil rarely drank to excess in college. He had, at the occasional party, enough beer to make him feel slightly intoxicated, but he never drank to the point that he lost control and he never drank hard liquor. Being sloppy drunk wasn't Neil's style. He didn't use drugs of any kind. Neil wanted to be an officer in the Marine Corps. He understood that while it was certainly okay to tie one on at a stateside party, in combat being drunk or high was absolutely unacceptable. Neil wanted to be an example to others who served, and so at parties, he kept his wits about him, often taking people home who were too drunk to drive and ensuring that none of the guys got too aggressive with the women present. Neil was respected by his friends and colleagues and admired for his level-headedness and leadership.

When Neil returned from his first tour of duty, he was a changed man. He was quiet and sullen. While at home, he rarely left his room except to go for long, solitary horseback rides. During family meals he tried to be upbeat, but found that he could not fake being happy. Nothing made him laugh. Not even his best friend could make him smile. It was a relief to everyone, Neil included, when he was redeployed. It was a difficult transition to go from combat to civilian life. He'd become acclimated to life as a Marine. In battle was where he wanted to be.

After Neil was wounded a second time and returned home, he was given large doses of prescription pain medications. These pills helped his physical pain, but they did not make him forget what he had witnessed in war. He was plagued by night terrors and diagnosed with post-traumatic stress disorder (PTSD). If anyone came up behind him too quickly, Neil would jump out of his skin. Sometimes he had to consciously stop himself from ripping an unsuspecting person's throat out. To calm down, he started to drink. Drinking, in combination with his pain medication, which he took in twice the prescribed dosage, allowed him to sleep as much as twelve hours a day. When he was awake, Neil described himself as feeling "dead inside." When Neil confessed to his father that he felt suicidal, his family persuaded him to go to the VA hospital, where he was put on suicide watch and later placed in a drug rehabilitation program.

Neil was unable to let his guard down in the VA program. "I just didn't like it," he said. "I knew they wanted to help me, but I didn't like the twelve-step aspect. You would doubt that God would help you, too, if you'd seen the things I have seen."

After two weeks, Neil left the VA program. His parents reached out to a private treatment center in California and asked for help for their son. Within forty-eight hours, Neil had a bed in that treatment center.

Realizing that Neil needed to work with a therapist who had been in the armed forces and specialized in the treatment of PTSD among veterans, the treatment center brought in a professional specifically to work with Neil. Neil met with this specialist three times a week in addition to his sessions with his therapist. Neil described his sessions with the military PTSD specialist as "the real deal." Finally, Neil believed he'd found someone who could understand him and his experiences. His specialist was tough. He'd witnessed unbelievable atrocities in Vietnam. But he also understood Neil's pain and could be soft in the moments Neil needed him to be. He taught Neil how to express his feelings and helped him to cry.

It was in Afghanistan that Neil's problems first began. While in Afghanistan, Neil led a group of Marines on a mission in a desolate area of the country. They camped near a small village. Late one afternoon, a young woman came running toward the Americans' camp. "I knew something was terribly wrong," Neil said. "Her burka was torn and her veil was missing. As she got closer, I realized that her clothing wasn't so much torn as eaten away. She'd had acid thrown on her." Aghast, Neil watched in horror as the woman ran toward him, shouting in her native language. On the trail behind her, Neil saw that she was being pursued. Neil and his men held their weapons at the ready and began shouting at both the woman and the man who was chasing her to stop. Neither responded. "And then, I heard the single shot," Neil said. The woman dropped to the ground dead. Her pursuer had shot her. When her body hit the ground, the man lowered his gun, grinned at the Americans, and left. He did not even bother to retrieve her body.

It was Neil and the other Marines who buried the woman. "I couldn't bear to watch the animals scavenge her," Neil said.

Neil learned later that the woman had been accused of adultery. Her husband levied the charge, though he had no evidence of her alleged betrayal. It was he who had thrown the acid on her in the street while the woman's brothers cheered him on. It was he who chased her down as she fled the village and shot her when he feared that the Americans might give her refuge.

This was not the only incident that troubled Neil. He continually witnessed the mistreatment of women and girls in Iraq and Afghanistan. "I felt helpless to do anything to help them," Neil said. Coming from the kind of close-knit family that he did with three older sisters, Neil was unaccustomed to what he considered blatant disrespect for girls and women. Neil didn't feel like an honorable man, fighting for the freedom of people in countries where women are publicly abused and murdered. None of it made sense. He could not always defend those in need. When he could not protect a girls' school from having its wells poisoned or being attacked with grenades, he felt awful. This was not what he had envisioned when he'd dreamed of being a Marine back in Texas. Yes, it was important to find and eliminate threats to American security, but Neil wondered what he was fighting for if he couldn't bring at least a little bit of the freedom US citizens enjoy to these countries. He hated watching women die.

Because Neil made an immediate connection with his PTSD specialist and his therapist, he was able to open up and take full advantage of everything treatment had to offer. He applied himself to his recovery as perhaps only a Marine can and needed only thirty-seven days in treatment to gain a true foothold on sobriety. Once back at home, Neil was referred to a therapist who could help him continue to work through the issues he had as a war veteran and process the horrors he'd seen, many of them far worse than watching the Afghan woman's murder. Neil also became an advocate for women's human rights. As part of his aftercare plan, Neil began to work with a nonprofit group that funds a girls' school in Kabul. Although it is a fight against mortal danger every day for the girls at the school to receive an education, the girls go. Neil is proud to fundraise in support of this effort, which he does in part to make up for his inability to act on the behalf of Afghan girls while he was in their country.

Neil has been sober for three years. He is married, works with his father as a contractor, and is expecting his first child.

5

The Evidence-Base

What Is the Evidence-Base?

The evidence-base for addiction treatment consists of all the techniques shown to improve an addict's chances of becoming sober and remaining sober. It is the totality of the industry's best practices, its combined experience of trying new treatments and learning what works best for most addicts. Data from research conducted by universities, government agencies, and independent organizations informs the evidence-base. The research is varied, giving us many sources from which to learn what works, what is as yet unproven, what shows promise, and what does not.

One type of data used to inform the evidence-base is the randomized clinical trial. This is the kind of research most often associated with pharmaceutical research. Here is one example of what can be learned from a clinical trial. If 1,000 clients participate in a clinical trial of medication X for depression, 500 might be given the medication and 500 a placebo. Neither group is given any other sort of medication or therapy. At the end of a pre-specified period, perhaps a year, we might find that those who were given medication X showed a 23 percent better depression recovery rate than those given the placebo. If this trial was done many times over by different researchers and all of them showed similar results, we could conclude that medication X improves a client's chances of overcoming depression more than no medication at all.

While randomized clinical trials are considered by some to be the most reliable form of research, they are not generally well-suited to addiction research. Behavioral disorders, such as addiction, are complex. It is difficult to isolate and look at a single variable involved in this type of disorder. The range of responses between clients to a particular treatment can be unbelievably wide due to a series of variables too great to control. In other words, a randomized clinical trial cannot determine why some addicts respond very well to twelve-step programs and others are entirely unable to maintain sobriety in such a setting. There are too many factors involved to give such a trial meaning because each addict's response to twelve-step programs is unique in unquantifiable ways. Randomized clinical trials rely on the identification of a single variable as the cause of the cure; that is tricky if not impossible to do when looking at complex behaviors like addiction.

The type of data most commonly used to create the evidence-base in addiction treatment is a consensus review of the available research. This means that many experts, ranging from researchers to physicians to addiction treatment professionals, look at all the research that is published about addiction and highlight themes or commonalities present in the data. The research they explore is wide-ranging. While it may include clinical trials, it also includes other types of research that provide insight into the processes of psychological and behavioral change.

It is important to make one point very clear; just because

the evidence-base suggests that a treatment is effective with a specific population group does not mean that it will work for any particular client. In the evidence-base, researchers take specific information and form general rules with it. No treatment, however well researched or commonly practiced, works for everyone. The evidence-base never suggests that every practice works for every person.

The evidence-base is useful in providing information to clinicians about which practices and treatments work with more clients most often. For example, talk therapies are considered extremely effective in addiction treatment. While addicts benefit from discussing their problems and struggles with others, not all will benefit from the same type of talk therapy. The vast majority of addicts will respond best to individual therapy, but there are those who will thrive with the accountability of a small group therapy session. Others may prefer more informal interactions, such as working with a life coach or member of the clergy, especially after their recovery is cemented. Most will probably benefit from any or all of these approaches to varying degrees. What we know is this: talk therapies help. If the addict is not in a setting in which professionals can assess which type of talk therapy will benefit him the most, he must choose what he feels is the best therapy to meet his needs.

Treatment Approaches That Work

In order to stay informed of the newest developments in addiction treatment, our staff members regularly read the scientific literature in a variety of fields, including medicine, psychology, complementary medical practices, and neuroscience. As our knowledge and understanding of addiction treatment grows, our treatment methods also evolve. Our clinical staff cumulatively has more than one hundred years of experience in addiction treatment, an outstanding achievement for a boutique facility as intimate as ours. This experience gives them a great deal of insight into what works with particular types of clients and what does not. Remember, the evidence-base can only deal in generalities; it tells us what works for some of the people some of the time. We use that general information as a starting point to give each client what he needs in particular in order to recover from his addiction based on his individual preferences and conditions.

There are, however, some clear, widely accepted rules of addiction treatment that will apply to most clients.

Long-Term Treatment
Is More Effective Than Short-Term Treatment

While there certainly are exceptions to the rule, most clients get the firmest hold on recovery with more than a twenty-eight day stint in treatment. Yes, there are those who come to treatment extremely motivated to recover and have the will to match that motivation. There are those who may have been to treatment before, relapsed, and need only a tune-up, some help in one particular area, to ground their recovery. There are the fortunate few who have a great deal of personal insight into why they became addicts and tremendous support systems outside of treatment that can help them remain sober. Addicts in these circumstances may thrive with only thirty days of treatment, but for most people this short amount of time isn't sufficient to prevent relapse.

At our facility, the average recommended stay is somewhere between forty-five and ninety days, though the actual length of stay is suggested on an individual basis. We do not tell clients before entering treatment that in thirty days they will be sober for good and the problems in their lives will be solved. That sort of assurance would be disingenuous. While other treatment centers may offer this kind of promise, we find it unacceptable and potentially dangerous.

Using history is one important factor that provides a good example of the kind or variance one sees between addicts. If a client had back surgery six months ago and found himself physically addicted to painkillers after a few months of use, thirty or forty-five days of treatment might be sufficient to cement recovery. On the other hand, if someone has been drinking from morning until night and consuming two pints of hard liquor a day for twenty years, it would be unreasonable to suggest that any treatment center could assist in creating long-term sobriety for this client in thirty days. So while length of stay is variable, expect something in the range of two to three months as the average at Cliffside Malibu.

How do we recommend a length of stay? It will be based on the addict's readiness and willingness to change, as well as his progress in treatment. We bring clients into treatment, give them the resources they need to get sober, and then make recommendations for therapeutic activities that will help each addict maintain his sobriety outside the treatment facility. This last step is commonly referred to as an aftercare plan. Our goal is to give every client the tools he needs to maintain lasting recovery from addiction once he leaves treatment. The length of stay required for that will vary from client to client.

Usually, the addict will be critical of the suggestion that

he needs to stay in treatment for more than thirty days. We have been told to expect thirty days of treatment to recover. This is not because addiction can be overcome in thirty days, but because twenty-eight to thirty days is commonly what insurance pays for. Lasting recovery takes much longer to cement. Our goal is to help addicts get sober and lead happy, productive lives. If a client stays in treatment for only four weeks, detox alone can take up a large part of his stay; this does not leave enough time for the intensive work most addicts require to maintain their recovery outside of treatment. Don't take our word for this. Read up on addiction. The evidence is clear—those who stay in treatment longer have a better chance of remaining clean outside of treatment than those who do not.

Mind-Body-Spirit Approaches

The evidence-base also suggests that mind-body-spirit, also known as holistic, approaches to addiction treatment are the most effective in developing lasting sobriety. During treatment, the emphasis placed on each area will change, but the mind, body, and spirit must all be addressed. For example, early in treatment, the most emphasis is often placed on the body. By paying special attention to the client's physical needs in the early days of treatment, we ensure that detox is as painless as possible. As the client begins to recover his physical health, more attention is given to the areas of mind and spirit.

What do we mean by mind, body, and spirit? The *mind* refers to the psyche, the addict's emotional and psychological health. Anxiety, depression, and psychological trauma are all conditions that primarily affect a person's mind. *Body* refers to a person's physical well-being. Conditions of the physical body can include injuries, malnutrition, damage done to organs from drug use, and chemical imbalances that result in physical or psychological disorders. *Spirit* is a more ambiguous term. While some use the term spirit to mean a religious path or metaphysical state, we use this term to reference hope. Do you believe change is possible? Do you have hope for your future? Do you believe in the potential for joy and living a full life? The process of understanding and answering questions such as these will help the addict understand his spiritual aspect.

The evidence-base clearly shows that addiction is not solely a physical, mental, or spiritual disorder. Any treatment center that claims otherwise is contradicting the data. There are programs that suggest that with a good detox, fresh air, exercise, and good nutrition, the addict will recover. There are other programs that focus almost entirely on psychology and on the addict's longstanding trauma, but do very little to address the addict's hopes and dreams (his spiritual needs). Dealing with the past is necessary, but an addict must have hope for the future in order to want recovery strongly enough to do what is required to achieve it. Finally, there are programs that suggest that a belief in specific religious principles or a particular teacher will "set you free." These programs also have high failure rates. Any program that focuses on only one aspect of a person's makeup will fail to ensure long-term recovery. Human beings are complex creatures with multiple needs. Each part of the person—mind, body, and spirit—must be addressed and treated if the addict is going to maintain his recovery.

While we focus strongly on processing past experiences and learning how to deal more successfully with feelings and difficult events in the future, we also incorporate treatments for the body and spirit such as massage, yoga, personal training, proper nutrition, orthomolecular therapies, journaling, meditation, and opportunities for spiritual development. Spiritual development might mean developing a meditative or yoga practice, attendance at twelve-step meetings, or a particular religious practice of the addict's choosing. There are no right or wrong approaches, only options based on the addict's preferences and needs. As discharge grows nearer, greater emphasis is placed on integrating all the changes the addict has put into place while in treatment, and we formulate ways in which these changes can become part of daily life outside the treatment facility.

Who You Work with Is As Important As What You Do

The evidence-base further suggests that the people involved in your treatment are equally or more important than the treatment activities themselves. An extremely talented therapist can help clients even in less than optimal circumstances, but a fantastic treatment protocol may not be effective if implemented by an inexperienced or untalented practitioner.

Hiring and retaining only the most competent, compassionate staff available in the field of addiction treatment is essential to the success of any facility. We employ qualified staff members who are completely dedicated to our clients' recovery. We only hire therapists who understand addiction intimately and are willing and able to help clients do the work required to transcend past traumatic events so that they may change their behavior and overcome addiction permanently. We also maintain a "boutique" setting. Cliffside Malibu has only a small number of beds, allowing each of our staff members to devote significant time and attention to each of our clients. We are committed entirely to meeting each client's needs. This is a critical component of any quality treatment program.

Treating Addiction's Root Causes

One of the reasons quick fixes and short-term stays in treatment usually don't help an addict maintain long-term recovery is that these limited efforts often fail to address the root causes of addiction. The addict must understand the reasons why he began to engage in addictive behaviors in the first place in order to recover.

Determining the root causes of addiction is in many ways influenced by the ways in which we define addiction. If we view addiction as a moral deficiency, for example, we believe that its root cause is moral turpitude (bad behavior based on poor values). This view has resulted in treatment plans that focus on shaming an addict into changing his behavior. In the 1700s, the pilgrims locked drunks in the stocks for the whole town to see and ridicule. This type of punishment is still used today. There are judges in the United States who force those convicted of petty crimes, such as public intoxication, to stand on street corners with a sign describing their crimes. This is a form of aversion therapy; the idea is to shame the person so much that he won't act the same way again. As you can imagine, such measures are largely ineffective.

We treat addiction from a behavioral viewpoint. We understand change as a process. Each client, when he is ready, must consider the situations, circumstances, events, or experiences that caused him to use drugs in the first place. Remember, we are not talking about an average person who uses a substance once in a while as a social lubricant or to enhance an interpersonal experience. The addict does not enjoy a glass of wine with dinner or getting a little tipsy to loosen inhibitions before a romantic encounter. We're not even talking about the person who gets a little carried away at a wedding or bachelor party and pays for the debauchery with a hangover the following day. An addict habitually and consistently abuses a substance or substances to the point that his life and health are damaged by their use. That kind of habit does not emerge out of the blue; it is almost always triggered by painful life circumstances.

Part of the deep psychological work we do in treatment is rooting out the primary causes of addiction that are unique to each client. This is why our protocols are highly personalized and based on regular interpersonal interaction with a qualified, compassionate therapist. Each client is provided with a trustworthy partner who can serve as a guide to the therapeutic work that needs to be done. This partner creates a treatment program designed to meet the needs of the addict, enabling him to develop skills and insight in the areas in which he is deficient. The therapist is the addict's guide to change, helping him through the stages of change process and helping him to make lifestyle choices that are meaningful and fulfilling. Treatment is always designed to be holistic and progressive, developing as the client does, so that the root causes that led to addictive behaviors are healed and the addict can change his lifestyle to create a sober life in which there is no need for him to return to addiction.

A Complete Change of Lifestyle

Addiction recovery requires a complete change of lifestyle. The addict enters treatment with a lifestyle that has destroyed his hope and is literally killing his body. In treatment, the addict learns how to live in a different, more fulfilling way. As the root causes of his trauma are healed and his body and mind become healthier, he finds more motivation to remain sober than he had in the past. After working through the process of change, the addict discovers that he no longer wants to return to his old lifestyle. He finally experiences what a good life really is. He is able to enjoy interactions with his friends, children, and family. He finds usefulness and purpose in his work. He is present and lively in social settings. Once change has been habituated, it actually becomes more of a challenge to relapse than it does to maintain a sober lifestyle. The overcoming of the root causes of addiction is the true path to long-term recovery and is available to those who make a complete change in their lives through treatment.

Changing the Brain

Perhaps the most important new evidence-based addiction findings come from neuroscience, the study of how the brain works. Neuroscientists are teaching us that the brain is much more dynamic than we had previously imagined, and it changes in response to how it is used. In fact, many scientists are now considering addiction a brain disorder rather than a genetic disease.

When addiction develops in the brain, it does so in part by creating new neural pathways. Imagine that you lift a weight over and over again. Your arm will become stronger as you exercise specific muscles. In the brain, when an addict uses drugs over and over again, new neural pathways develop—not unlike new muscle developing when a person lifts weights. In other words, the brain develops a "let's use drugs" pattern. This pattern becomes so well developed that it begins to override other thought processes until the addict literally cannot choose another behavior. Research in the form of brain scans is now coming out of many different universities to support this idea.

When this concept of "neuroplasticity" is applied to addiction treatment, we find that just as addiction develops new neural pathways—what we call an "addiction feedback loop"—so too can addiction treatment develop new neural pathways, or a "recovery feedback loop." Thus in treatment, we use a variety of different therapies—biological, psychological, and spiritual—to stimulate the brain into building new neural pathways. This ingrains recovery into the brain until it literally becomes the way a person lives. While the old addiction feedback loop is always present, if it is not used, it withers just as the muscle that is not exercised atrophies. At the same time, the recovery feedback loop gets more attention and continues to develop and grow stronger.

Addict in Recovery: Mia Buckley

When thirty-five-year-old Mia Buckley walked into the treatment center, she was completely demoralized. She bore the weight of every judgment anyone's ever given a junkie mother. "I love my son, but I don't deserve him," she said often in her first weeks in treatment. Mia had done things to her son that she believed were unpardonable. She had taken him with her to a dealer's house when she needed to buy drugs. She left him in the car on street corners while she made buys. She even breastfed her son immediately after shooting heroin, later checking on him every few minutes, terror-stricken that he might stop breathing as a result of ingesting too much of the drug through her breast milk. Because of this, Mia was not initially a great candidate for recovery. An addict has to be able to move on from her past, even the mistakes she considers unforgiveable, if she is to have any hope of a future.

Mia's life wasn't always this dismal. She was born in Los Angeles to a respected couple. Her mother was a well-known university professor. The man she knew as her father was a charming business owner who sold and restored antique art prints. Both her parents adored her, and still do.

Mia's stepfather had adopted her. Her biological father was a shadowy figure plagued by alcoholism whom she hardly knew. He rarely called or sent letters to his daughter; he knew that she had a wonderful, loving father figure and so stayed away. When Mia was eleven, her biological father died of complications from alcoholism.

Still, as a child, Mia was relatively happy. An only child, Mia's parents showered her with attention. She attended good private schools and participated in an array of extracurricular activities. Additionally, she was able to travel with her mother to conferences, speak with crowds of intelligent people associated with the university, and attend art exhibits and theater productions on campus. Mia was cultured, smart, and on a positive track for the future.

However, Mia liked to get high—a lot. In high school, she would sit in the back parking lot, smoke cigarettes, and pop pills. Prescription pain pills and anti-anxiety medications were her favorites, though she'd take whatever was available. Later, she progressed to heroin, though she refused to shoot the drug. "I never used needles then," Mia said when sharing her story. "I thought I was being smart by only smoking or snorting the heroin. It didn't seem like a problem to me so long as I didn't shoot it. I didn't see myself as a junkie."

Mia had a passion for writing. She attended a very well-regarded undergraduate university, then completed a master's of fine arts from a prestigious film-writing program. Her parents were beyond proud! They helped her find a small bungalow near Venice Beach where she set out to write the next blockbuster Hollywood hit. But she was taking too much heroin to get anything accomplished on her screenplay. Time and again, Mia's parents would come to visit only to find her passed out at her writing table or on the floor or in the bathroom. They insisted that she go to treatment. She did. She got sober and went back to her writing.

Unfortunately, Mia was not able to stay sober for more than a couple of years at a time. She tried, but the ghosts of her past always haunted her. Though she did not want to admit it because she loved her mother and stepfather dearly, she felt a deep sense of loss in never having a relationship with her biological father. She thought of him often, especially at milestone events. The fact that he died of the same problem that she struggled with consumed her. Mia knew that her father was an artist and imagined that he had been a creative and sensitive person as she was. She wondered if it had caused him pain to have a daughter whom he couldn't see, knowing his alcoholism would only hurt her. Mia would dream about her father, write to her father, have conversations with him in her mind, and, eventually, when she became sad enough from all her mental conjuring of him, she'd slip into a clinical depression. Taking heroin seemed to be the only way to stop the pain. Her binges would last a few months and then she'd go to rehab. It was a vicious cycle.

In one of her sober periods, Mia met and married a man she hoped to spend the rest of her life with. He moved into her bungalow by the beach. Their marriage was solid, and they lived together peacefully, Mia working on her writing all the while.

Then, Mia was involved in a car accident. She suffered a severe spinal injury that doctors feared would leave her paralyzed. Many surgeries and a year of physical therapy later, Mia was able to walk, but was in constant pain. Her doctor prescribed OxyContin. Mia took the pills gratefully. She believed that because her pain was physical, she would be able to control how much of the pain medication she used. She did not consider her drug use a relapse.

The drugs worked on the pain and on Mia's depression. Her husband noticed that she was more talkative and energetic than she'd ever been before. They both attributed this change to her pain being gone and not to her drug use.

When the pain clinic began to reduce Mia's dose, her depression returned. Though the physical pain was almost entirely gone, her energy level was low. She didn't feel happy or talkative without the OxyContin, so she did what any addict would do. She lied. She went back to the pain clinic and said that her pain had returned worse than ever. Her doctor was concerned and wanted to run more tests. Feeling guilty, Mia cancelled the appointment for these tests. The pain clinic dropped her as a patient. Feeling as if she would die if she did not get her drugs, Mia began "doctor shopping," moving from physician to physician with made-up ailments trying to secure prescriptions for the drugs she wanted. Though she was disgusted by her own behavior, she didn't believe she had any other options. She needed her drugs to live.

One of the last times Mia was in rehab, she met a woman who taught her how to melt her painkillers and shoot them intravenously. This was the beginning of a terrible downward spiral. Mia simply could not stop using at all once she started shooting painkillers.

Then Mia got pregnant. Horrified that she would damage her unborn child, she was honest with her obstetrician about her drug use. He helped her draw down her dose to a level that would not harm the fetus, but was also enough that Mia would not be unduly stressed during her pregnancy. Fortunately, Mia was able to follow her doctor's instructions and gave birth to a healthy baby boy. After she recovered from her C-section, the obstetrician began to lower her dosage of painkillers. Mia was told that the levels of medication she was on were not high enough to harm her son if she breastfed him, so she did. Looking into her son's beautiful face, Mia was sure that she would never use again.

Of course, the day Mia's prescription for pain medication ran out, she was back on the phone with the friend who had taught her how to shoot drugs. That friend had moved on to heroin. Although the thought of returning to street drugs horrified Mia, she bought the heroin anyway. Accustomed to shooting her painkillers, Mia knew that she now needed to shoot the heroin for it to have any real effect. However, she was aghast to realize that the OxyContin she had been shooting was much stronger than the heroin. It was actually a reduction in the level of her drug use to use street drugs instead of pharmaceuticals! Still, she was an addict, and she felt she had no choice but to use. She considered herself the lowest of the low, a junkie who put her child in danger so that she could score. If it weren't for the love she had for her son, Mia might have killed herself.

Richard Taite knew Mia casually through mutual friends. When he saw her at an event, obviously strung out but doing her best to hide it, he offered her a place in treatment. Richard promised Mia that she could recover and, while she didn't believe him, she gave treatment another chance for her son's sake.

Mia stayed in treatment for just over three months. At first, she could not forgive herself for using after she had her son. She spent weeks in treatment thinking about recovery, but unable to move toward change because she believed herself to be reprehensible in every way for being a junkie mom. Mia's therapist and Richard would not give up on her even when Mia wanted to quit on herself. They talked to her time and time again about self-forgiveness. Eventually she heard what her therapist had been saying to her for weeks, "If you're going to be the mother your son needs, you have to be that mother now and every day you still have on this Earth." Mia thought about her own father, recognizing the pain he must have felt being away from her. She didn't want to follow in his footsteps. From that moment, the moment she chose to be her son's mother above all else, Mia's recovery clicked into place. She was easily able to follow the course of action laid before her. Change from that point on was fast paced. It wasn't long before Mia was sober and able to return home to her husband and son.

Mia has been sober for more than four years. Her son hardly remembers the three months she spent away from him.

6

Stages of Change

In this chapter we will describe the Stages of Change model, a well-proven psychological approach to change that helps addicts replace addictive behaviors with healthy habits. One of this model's strong points is that therapists who understand the stages of change are able to meet addicts at any level of willingness to change their behaviors, from complete denial that a problem exists to excitement and readiness to make lifestyle changes. Our therapists meet regularly with their clients to guide them through each stage of change, enabling them to achieve solid, long-term recovery from addiction.

The Philosophy of Meeting People Where They Are

Psychology is a fragmented field. There is no real consensus on the reasons for psychological distress or the ways in which that distress should best be treated. Because of this, psychological treatments vary widely. There are many schools of thought about why people have problems and what to do to help them overcome those problems. A Jungian trained therapist will treat clients very differently than a cognitive behavioral therapist. In either case, however, the therapist will try to fit the client's symptoms or issues into a theoretical framework based on his training and expertise. In other words, the client will receive the treatment the therapist was trained to give; this is not necessarily the most effective treatment for the client.

Dr. James Prochaska, at the University of Rhode Island, found this situation of fragmentation to be a problem for psychology. How were people going to overcome their problems if there was no agreement on how to treat them? In order to find an answer to this question, Prochaska began to research processes of change. He and his colleagues found that while different theories of psychology explained the underlying causes of problems in different ways, there was a general consensus on how change is created in the individual. In other words, therapists don't agree on why people have the issues that they have, but they do agree on some fundamental tools to help them overcome these issues. Prochaska described these steps and named them "Processes of Change."

The nine major processes of change are described beautifully in *Changing for Good*, a book written by Drs. Prochaska, Norcross, and DiClemente in 1994, and is still widely available. These processes of change are consciousness-raising, social liberation, emotional arousal, self-reevaluation, commitment, countering, environmental control, reward, and helping relationships. Each process is an important therapeutic tool that can be used to help clients overcome addiction. The key to successfully using each tool is for the therapist to know when and how to employ each process of change. To use the right tools at the right time, the therapist must correctly gauge a client's readiness for change. He must know which stage of change the client is in.

Prochaska and his colleagues suggested to therapists that in order to use these processes of change most effectively to help their clients, therapists had to have the ability to integrate treatment across theoretical schools. This idea is called the "Transtheoretical Model" of psychology. Therapists using a transtheoretical approach need to understand and be able to employ tools from the major psychological theories in order to use the strongest treatment techniques from each theory at the right time for each client. These techniques are chosen based on the client's openness and readiness to make life changes. Prochaska and his team described this method of moving a client through the steps associated with change and named the process Stages of Change.

Cliffside Malibu therapists use the Stages of Change model to help every client overcome addiction. We do this because we recognize that people need to be met at their individual stage of change or readiness to change. There are addicts who are sent to treatment who truly have no idea that they have a problem with alcohol and drugs. There are other addicts who can't wait to get to treatment because they are extremely motivated to put their addiction behind them. Some are aware of the reasons they use drugs or alcohol. Others have no idea why they can't stop using. Some have made good progress toward quitting before they come to treatment. Others can't imagine life without alcohol or drugs. It makes absolutely no difference which stage the addict is in when he enters treatment. What matters is that the clinical staff of the treatment center can identify and work with the addict at whatever level of readiness for change he finds himself. Change is possible.

The Stages of Change

Prochaska and his team identified six well-defined stages of change. They are precontemplation, contemplation, preparation, action, maintenance, and termination. Each of these stages will be described briefly in this chapter. For a more comprehensive look at each of these stages and of the Stages of Change model as a whole, please read *Changing for Good*, the book in which Drs. Prochaska, Norcross, and DiClemente present the model in depth.

Precontemplation

I was smoking crack every day. I didn't eat or sleep and I only left my apartment to meet the dealer. Then one day, I answered the door and my whole family was there. They were concerned and each had a letter to read to me about how worried they were and how I was going to die if I didn't change my life. All I kept thinking was, "What are you talking about?"

Addicts in the precontemplation stage are easy to identify. Their mindset is characterized by denial and/or demoralization. This is the addict who sees nothing wrong with his drinking even though he's been in front of the judge twice in the past three months for driving while intoxicated. He isn't a drunk; he's just got bad luck. Alternatively, addicts in the precontemplation stage sometimes know that they are addicts, but feel powerless to do anything to change. These are the addicts resigned to the pain, suffering, and degradation that go along with being an addict. These addicts often don't even try to hide their addiction. There is no point for they have no hope.

Some addicts in the precontemplation stage may not be consciously aware of their thoughts about their addiction. They are invested in staying unaware of their problem and often act out if confronted. Consider the middle-aged woman who never in her life shows a tendency toward addiction until she is given opioid pain medication after shoulder surgery. If she begins abusing the medication and becomes addicted to it, it is likely that her friends and family will recognize her problem long before she does. If confronted, she will probably storm out of the room. She cannot and will not face her addiction because the reality of her dependency is too overwhelming to accept.

By ignoring a problem, an addict can stay safely insulated from reality. He can feel safe in the knowledge that he can't fail because he doesn't need to make any effort to change. He can deny feelings of guilt because, if there is no problem, he has not done anything wrong. Ignoring a problem makes it feel like an illusion. If there's only an illusion of a problem, there's no reason for concern. Most significantly, if there is no problem, there is no reason to change. Change can be terrifying for an addict, especially if he has any hint of the depth of his addiction.

Often, the addict in the precontemplation stage of change blames his friends and family for his problems. When confronted with his own unacceptable behavior, he may create a scene in an effort to chase people away. Meddling family, friends, the police, bosses, and doctors are the real issues, not substance abuse. An addict in this mindset will do everything he can to avoid facing the reality of his situation.

To identify an addict in the precontemplation stage of change, consider the following questions.

- Does the person I care for deny or downplay his behavior? Does he say things like "I don't drink that much" or "I only get high when I go out" to minimize his behavior?

- Am I constantly given excuses and rationalizations for why my loved one's addiction is more important than his social, familial, or financial obligations?

- Does the addict in my life blame me or others for his problems?

- Is the person I care for unable to express negative feelings? Are there real, difficult situations in his life that he treats with alcohol or drugs instead of asking for support from his friends and family or seeking professional help?

Addicts in the precontemplation stage of change will generally exhibit some or all of the characteristics listed above. If you answered yes to any of these questions, the addict in your life may be at the precontemplation stage of change.

Those who recognize their addiction, but feel powerless to change, will often behave as if they are in denial. However, in moments of clarity or honesty, the addict will share his demoralization. This addict is resigned to die an addict's death. He feels defeated. He is the street junkie who has lost all direction, the man who sits alone day in and day out at the bar, and the actor who once had his choice of jobs but now cannot get hired because he's too much trouble. This addict may have tried to stop using on his own, but failed.

Even though he knows a problem exists, he does not believe change is possible.

Addicts in the precontemplation stage of change do not get better without help. They do not have the inner resources to attempt to overcome their addictions. Even those who want to get sober will give up when the withdrawal symptoms become too great. This is no different than someone who wants to stop smoking cigarettes, but cannot last even one day because the nicotine cravings are so strong. In isolation, without support of any kind, those in the precontemplation stage of change are unlikely to succeed.

Addicts in the precontemplation stage of change are excellent prospects for treatment. They can and do recover. How do we get their attention? Many people suggest that we should wait for the addict to "hit bottom," to destroy his life to such an extent that he can't help but realize that something is wrong and that he needs help. Waiting for someone to hit bottom is a risky proposition. While we are waiting, the addict may sustain irreparable damage to his health and life. He may drive while intoxicated and kill someone. He may overdose one too many times and end up dead. We know that medical problems are treated much more effectively when they are less severe. This is the obvious case for cancer. We don't wait until the cancer fully develops before we treat it. We treat it as soon as we see the first signs. Addiction is no different. In approaching the addict in the precontemplation stage, we help him develop an understanding of his problem so that he may not have to destroy his life and health completely before getting treatment. In some cases, this can be done in an intervention and in others, through work in treatment.

Helping those in the precontemplation stage of change

requires the use of three different tools: consciousness raising, building helping relationships, and social liberation. Consciousness raising involves helping the addict become aware that addiction is a problem. The addict needs help to see how his addiction affects his life and the lives of others. Building helping relationships refers to assisting the addict as he begins to recognize his need for help. Many addicts, especially those in denial, push friends and family away; they may no longer have the relationships they need to sustain change outside of treatment. We begin to help the addict build the support system he will need to make recovery lasting. Finally, social liberation is the process of providing healthy choices for the addict and offering support during the change process. Often, families and friends are not capable of providing that support. In these situations, not only is a dedicated and caring therapist a necessity, but support groups should also be considered so the addict has many people to reach out to in times of need.

Precontemplation is the first stage of the change process. Recovery is just around the corner for these addicts even though they do not yet realize it.

Contemplation

I knew that sometimes I drank too much, but I could always sober up when I needed to. It wasn't a problem for me because I could control it. Then one morning I woke up in a strange hotel. As soon as I got out of bed I felt sick and barely made it to the bathroom in time to vomit. I had no idea where I was or how I had gotten there. At that point I began to think that I might have a problem with alcohol.

In the contemplation stage of change, the addict substitutes thinking for acting. This is the addict who talks and talks about his problems, often resolutely stating that he wants to change, but never does a thing to set or reach any goals. Those who are contemplating change definitely want the change to happen, but are ambivalent about taking any steps toward making the change a reality. They have a dream rather than a goal.

Addicts in the contemplation stage of change outside of treatment run the risk of getting stuck there. There are many reasons why someone in the contemplation stage might become frozen. Most notably, action brings fear of failure. Who hasn't felt anxiety in the face of trying to make a change? We've all been there. Imagine that you want to lose ten pounds. You'd love to lose ten pounds. Your clothes would fit better and your health might improve a bit. But it's hard to lose weight. And tonight, your spouse is taking you out to a really nice restaurant for dinner. Besides, you don't look that bad. Before you know it, you're home and feeling a little ill from having eaten the entire bread basket and though you're appalled to admit it even to yourself, you had to undo the top button on your pants in the car. Yet, by morning, you're feeling better and have a new excuse that will keep you from changing your eating habits. This mindset characterizes a person in the contemplation stage of change. The addict cannot fail if he does not try. Meanwhile, he receives whatever payoff he gets from continuing to practice his addiction.

Those in the contemplation stage want certainty. They want to know that they will definitely succeed in their efforts to change. But they also don't want to make any big sacrifices. This addict wants the change without the work.

"Wouldn't it be wonderful to wake up sober?" the addict might ask himself. Indeed, it would! However, to wake up sober and have it be a positive experience, the addict must face and resolve the issues that cause him to use in the first place. The addict in the contemplation stage of change believes the kind of work it would take to examine the root causes of his addiction is too difficult, and he isn't interested in doing it.

When anyone is trying to change a major behavior, whether it is addiction or anything else, there is a fear that change will be difficult. If you are attempting to change on your own, what Prochaska calls a "self-changer," this can be true. Losing even a modest amount of weight, for example, is hard when you're at home faced with the kids asking for macaroni and cheese and an emergency lunch meeting that forced you to cancel your exercise session and eat something from a vending machine. Temptation and obstacles are everywhere. Even those dedicated to change can get overwhelmed and give up in such circumstances.

Changing in a treatment center is an entirely different matter. Obstacles to change and temptations are removed. Every aspect of the addict's day is geared toward creating a successful path to a healthy, addiction-free life. Nutritious meals are prepared and served; time for exercise, personal contemplation, and therapy is provided; each client is paired with a committed, caring therapist who will lead him through the stages of change, offer a shoulder to cry on, and act as a cheering section; the client receives massages and personal training, and can get a haircut or manicure. We have housekeepers to keep our facility spotless and our clients are not required to do chores. We don't treat clients like children by taking away their phones or Internet privileges, but instead empower them to make healthy choices every minute of the day. The addict's only job is to work on himself. Every tool he needs to change his life is provided. Change will take time and commitment, but not the expected pain. The addict will come to realize that a sober life is a joyful life. This success will propel the addict forward, deepening his commitment to recovery.

The strong desire for change exhibited by those in the contemplation stage of change means that they are often very willing to talk about their problems. This willingness to share honestly is fantastic for treatment. Contemplators of change who are stuck in this stage may seem like they are repeating themselves for no reason, but what they are really looking for in the endless retelling of their stories is reassurance that change is possible. The therapist and others at the treatment center can provide this reassurance. The addict feels a restored sense of hope.

Sometimes, when an addict in the contemplation stage gets a good dose of hope, he will jump prematurely to action, undertaking changes without a plan. He has not yet acquired the tools he needs to succeed. This is like the morbidly obese man who has not exercised in more than ten years showing up to a marathon and saying, "Let's do this thing!" Of course he will not complete the task. Addicts in the contemplation stage bring this kind of energy to change. In treatment, this enthusiasm can be channeled in positive ways, helping the addict move solidly into the next stage of change. In the next stage, he will create a plan that will allow him to live the life he's begun to dream of outside the relative safety of the treatment center.

We use three tools when helping those in the contemplation stage of change: emotional arousal, consciousness raising, and self-reevaluation.

Emotional arousal is a tool that uses emotions to provide the energy required to overcome procrastination. Emotional arousal may come from a dramatic, emotionally charged event, like an intervention or a car wreck. In these moments, the addict reaches a tipping point. He suddenly wants change more than he fears failure. A therapist can use the addict's newfound desire to change to help him break through ambivalence and make a true commitment to action.

Consciousness raising in the contemplation stage of change is different than in the precontemplation stage. Consciousness raising in precontemplation is about helping the addict to see that a problem exists. In the contemplation stage of change, consciousness raising refers to helping the addict understand the nature of his problems. The addict does not understand the extent of his problems or their social, emotional, physical, and economic costs. To help the addict understand why he does what he does and see that other options are available, therapists, family, and friends should ask questions that provide informative responses. In this way, the addict can collect good data about his problems so that he can track changes and monitor both setbacks and progress. Similarly, in raising consciousness around addiction, we ask the addict to document what happens immediately prior to or after an event of problem behavior. For instance, we might ask the addict to recount a binge that had particularly disastrous consequences. Can the addict identify anything that caused this binge to be worse than others? Was anything done during or after the episode that made the consequences worse than they might have been otherwise? This kind of questioning helps the addict understand both his triggers and the consequences of his actions. Once the addict recognizes his triggers, he can make plans to avoid them whenever possible and figure out ways to handle them when they are unavoidable.

Self-reevaluation is a tool that allows addicts to reflect on themselves, their values, and the way they live their lives. When addicts in the contemplation stage of change use the self-reevaluation tool, they often learn that their values are in conflict with their problem behavior. An addict might say he loves his children, but when he drinks, his children are no longer his priority. This can be a heartbreaking realization for the addict and may give him the emotional impetus to make real change. Self-reevaluation helps addicts make these important connections between actions and consequences. With this information, addicts begin to realize that their lives would improve without the problem behavior. The addict begins to believe there is hope and takes concrete steps toward his new lifestyle.

The contemplation stage of change can feel almost magical to the addict. As he works with his therapist, old trauma is healed. The issues that drove his addictive behavior are lessened and eventually resolved. Pain is released. Facing the root causes that triggered his addictive behavior and finding liberation from them, the addict will find that his desire to use diminishes. As that occurs, he starts to see that a fulfilling, sober life is possible. He feels a strong emotional energy and a drive to make his positive life changes permanent.

Preparation

I finally saw that the way I was living my life wasn't working. I had to change and I had to change now! I needed to get help so I could learn the most effective way to change my life and then I needed to do it.

The preparation stage of change is the part of the change process in which the addict becomes ready to take action. The addict in this stage wants recovery and knows change is possible. He has begun to imagine a sober life for himself. He has gotten a taste of what it is like to feel better about himself, and he likes it. He is confident and willing to face the obstacles that will inevitably come. Now is the time to create a strategy that will help him succeed at changing his life in such a way that he can maintain his sobriety long-term.

Because there are many social, financial, and medical complications involved in leading an addiction-filled life, a solid action plan is necessary to move the addict from contemplation to action. If the addict skips the preparation stage, he is likely to fail. The enthusiasm for change created in the contemplation stage will not see the addict through to action. In the contemplation stage of change, the addict wants change, but not strongly enough to face the big challenges necessary to make that change. In the preparation stage, the addict's desire for action outweighs his comfort with the status quo, and he is willing to prepare to face any obstacle that stands in the way of making true lifestyle changes. The addict becomes willing to take the small action steps that will bring about that change.

Many addicts want to leap over the preparation stage of change and go directly from contemplation to action. At the moment the addict leaves the contemplation stage, he is usually emotionally motivated and energized. Unfortunately, this energy does not last. Premature action, or action without preparation, almost always leads to ineffective change. The preparation stage of change provides the addict the necessary time he needs to increase his confidence in his decision to change. This period of preparation gives the addict time to think about the physical and emotional pitfalls that may be ahead and how to handle interpersonal situations in a way that will not cause harmful repercussions. The preparation stage of change helps the addict to begin to think about others and incorporate their needs into his plan for sobriety.

An addict in the preparation stage of change continues to use the tool of self-reevaluation in his recovery plan. He focuses on the future, imagines his new self, and dreams about his healthy life. He must contemplate the improvements he wants in his life and remember these ideals in the tough times that are sure to come. This phase of preparation is exciting for the addict; the mind-numbing, downward spiral of addiction is really over. Now, the addict can dream! He can share and cultivate the best parts of himself and create a life he never before thought possible. Through positive visualization and goal setting, the addict begins to turn away from old behaviors and make sobriety a priority.

The addict in the preparation stage of change also uses the tool of commitment. He has overcome ambivalence, but he must be prepared for the anxiety he will face, especially once he is out of the treatment center and maintaining his recovery on his own. He has to continue wanting to be sober even in trying situations. We encourage the addict to take small steps and recognize that life change happens incrementally. Most importantly, he will create a plan of action that will set his new, healthy lifestyle on a solid foundation. He will have new ideas of what to do in tough situations or when interacting with difficult people.

As the addict prepares for action, he will need a great deal of support from his therapist, friends, and family. There will be times when his commitment to sobriety will lag. He will have bad days, disappointments, and setbacks that could open the door for relapse if he is unprepared. Friends, family, his therapist, and others can provide support in times of insecurity so that the addict does not become discouraged. Whenever the addict is faced with an obstacle, remind him that change is possible and that his new life awaits. He has envisioned his life free of addiction and is now beginning to experience it. This kind of loving support will see him through the rough patches.

Action

> *I started to feel better about my future. I was putting into practice the changes I had learned in therapy and my self-esteem was growing. Opportunities just started to pop up for me. I felt happier and more optimistic than I had in a long time.*

In the action stage of change the addict is propelled from one life to another. No longer cocooned in the relative safety of a treatment center, the addict implements his action plan when he returns home. He and his therapist have created this action plan so that he is set up for success. In treatment, it is easy to remain sober. After treatment, we help the addict arrange his days so that sober living is the norm. Now that the addict is out of the treatment facility, he begins to experience the real joys of living. He stays committed to the idea that using drugs is no longer an option.

No other stage is as busy as this stage of change. The addict in the action stage will consistently work to implement the plans he made during the preparation stage.

For some addicts, this is the stage in which relapse is the most likely. This is especially true for those who do not have the benefit of treatment and a good support system at home. For those addicts who complete treatment at Cliffside Malibu, relapse is rare. We provide a secure setting so that our clients can become comfortable with their lifestyle changes. These changes are reinforced in the addict's life outside treatment. We also help the addict develop his support system and identify any problematic relationships so that even if he has the impulse to relapse, he will find that his new habits and lifestyle prevent him from returning fully to his old behaviors. The addict now has too much information about addiction and himself to choose to engage in the devastating behavior he has successfully put behind him. He can no longer deny that he has a problem or blame the consequences of his using on others. He also likes his new life a lot and knows that he risks losing it if he returns to using. This inability to enjoy his addiction in his new life may be one of the reasons the addict usually picks himself up again after a relapse, if one occurs.

In order to progress effectively through the action stage of change, the addict is prepared in treatment to expect successful recovery and a fulfilling life. This expectation will help him through the inevitable anxiety and temptations that he will experience upon leaving treatment. At this stage, the addict knows that he will face challenges, but he is committed to his new life and knows he has the tools to overcome adversity without the use of drugs. He wants to achieve the vision he had for himself in the preparation stage, and he is prepared to do whatever it takes to manifest his vision.

There is no single right technique the addict can use to be successful in the action stage of change. Addicts in this stage of recovery are encouraged to use what works for them and substitute positive behaviors for negative ones. Some will find great solace in religion and replace substances with church attendance. Others will make a commitment to personal health and find comfort in exercise or yoga. There will be those who find support in the company of other addicts in recovery. Still others may find or return to a hobby that brings them great joy. When the addict engages in activities that bring him a sense of fulfillment and purpose, he finds that his relationships improve. He becomes more present in his life and realizes that he enjoys the little things that he did not even notice when he was using. Life becomes beautiful. Relapse seems unfathomable; he has too much to lose to return to his old behaviors.

The addict will use all his tools and resources in the action stage of change. However, in addition to relying on helping relationships, the three most notable tools are: countering, environmental control, and reward.

Countering is the substitution of healthy activities and responses for problem behaviors. There will always be circumstances, particularly early in sobriety, when the addict feels triggered and wants to use. An unanticipated circumstance, such as a legal problem, might trigger the addict's desire to use. Being sued, for example, certainly could make anyone want to escape reality by using a substance. A trigger might also occur at a particular time of day. If the addict poured himself a drink every day at six, he will probably still want a drink at six when he leaves treatment. With countering, the addict chooses not to use and instead does something good for himself. He might distract himself with work so that he doesn't think about his legal problems. He might begin exercising at what used to be his regular drinking time. He could practice meditation or relaxation techniques when he becomes stressed. There are many things the addict can do to replace addictive responses with healthy choices.

Part of the countering process is also to replace troubling thoughts with positive ones. An addict's self-talk is very often demoralizing. Self-doubt will creep into his mind. Addicts will tell themselves that they are awful people even when they act nobly. They will find the one flaw in a wonderful presentation and admonish themselves for it. Addicts also tell themselves that they will fail at recovery. These kinds of thoughts are the normal machinations of an addictive mind, and the addict must learn to be aware of this kind of thinking so that he can counter the negative with the positive. The addict's mind is negative when unguarded, yet he has the power to change his thoughts whenever he likes.

Countering also involves being assertive with those people in the addict's life who are not supportive of his recovery. Obviously, the addict's dealer and other people involved in his using life have an interest in seeing him remain addicted; those people can easily be eliminated from his new life. There are others who may not even be aware of their need to keep the addict unwell. The addict may have a parent who has become so accustomed to taking care of him that she no longer realizes she is making his addiction worse. His children may resent his sudden re-emergence in their lives; perhaps when the addict was using, his children had a lot of freedom and now they must obey rules. His coworkers with ambitions to replace him may be angered by his newfound productivity. In all these cases, the addict must be assertive and protect his recovery and suggest treatment for those he loves if it is appropriate.

Environmental control is another important tool used during the action stage of change. Environmental control means limiting access to dangerous people, places, or things. If there is no reason to go into a bar other than to drink, don't go in. If the addict's supervisor's sixtieth birthday party is being held at a swanky venue with an open bar, make a plan for how to deal with that temptation. If the addict says that he doesn't feel comfortable bowling because he cannot do it without getting loaded, try miniature golf. In any situation, the goal is to recognize triggers and have plans for how to deal with them. Have a list of positive behaviors that the addict can turn to when he finds himself in dangerous situations. Most importantly, if the addict finds he cannot control his behavior in an environment, he must remember that he is free to leave.

The reward tool that is used in the action stage transforms consequences by helping the addict make new choices. In other words, addicts feel better about themselves when they use self-reinforcing language and act with integrity. "Covert management" involves the addict giving himself pats on the back. Addicts tend to berate themselves terribly, even when they have acted healthfully and responsibly. Addicts using the reward tool learn to be kind to themselves when they make a mistake. This is extremely difficult for addicts to do. One means of helping addicts learn the reward skill is to ask them to think of how their favorite role models would respond to a certain situation or behavior. What would a beloved teacher, coach, manager, or family member say in this situation? With a step-by-step approach to recovery, applause for small improvements, and a strong foundation in the earlier stages of change, the addict can learn to appreciate and be proud of his achievements.

Helping relationships evolve in the action stage of change and remain vital to the addict's successful recovery. Outside the treatment center, the addict will require the assistance of a good therapist to support him as he continues to clean up the fallout of his addiction and navigate the difficulties of his new sober life. He may build relationships with sobriety buddies, others who are also recreating their lives around recovery. No matter what kind of support the addict chooses, it is a very good idea to expand his support network at this juncture of his recovery.

How does a recovering addict expand his support network? He might begin by writing down what he needs from friends, family, his therapist, and other concerned people in his life. He might seek out a support group if he does not have adequate support at home. Most importantly, he should do his best to remain positive and ask for positive reinforcement from others. In this stage, the addict needs to be strongly reminded that despite the anxiety and setbacks he may encounter, recovery is not only possible, it's worth the effort.

Maintenance

Today, I have a good life. There are still challenges, but now I know how to deal with them. I do not get stuck in problems, and I do not turn to drugs and alcohol as a solution. I have found purpose and joy in my life, and I know that in order to keep living this kind of life, I must keep practicing the new habits that I have been taught.

In the maintenance stage of change, the addict has made his new, sober lifestyle the norm. Though it is still possible to fall back into old habits, with long-term effort and a changed lifestyle, recovery will be the addict's "new normal." He will go to therapy, exercise, and choose healthier foods. These are his new habits; this is how he lives his new life.

If the addict does not enter and become adept at the maintenance stage of change, he becomes like the dieter who initially loses weight, but gains it all back the moment the diet is over. Action without maintenance is a Band-Aid solution to an entrenched problem. Addiction recovery only occurs when the addict has a strategy for long-term success. Quality addiction treatment can provide that strategy for success. The addict will learn how to find the energy, time, and dedication to execute his recovery plan on a daily basis. He will be motivated to make whatever changes are necessary to prevent a return to his addiction, and he will take those actions every day because he now knows how good it feels to be sober.

The maintenance stage of change builds on previous successes. Again, we cannot stress enough that successful maintenance literally means a brand new, healthy lifestyle for the addict. The addict will enjoy his new life; that's what keeps him sober. Finding fulfillment in spending time with family and friends, improved health, and clarity of mind is what cements the addict's recovery. The pleasure of his new life becomes so great that a return to his old life becomes unthinkable.

It is in the maintenance stage that the changes in the addict's brain are becoming strong—the recovery feedback loop is being developed. As time passes and the addict's habituated behavior becomes healthy, his brain directs him to continue with the healthy behavior. If you regularly exercise and then cannot for a day or two for some unexpected reason, you'll feel down and want to get back to your regular exercise program. Recovery is no different. In the maintenance stage, the addict will become comfortable with his healthier lifestyle and will default to it because it feels good and it is what his brain expects him to do.

Even in the midst of this new and wonderful life, relapse is possible. Addicts who have enjoyed years, even decades, of sober living have returned to their addictions. What causes relapse among those who have firmly committed them-selves to a sober way of life? The answer to that question is not simple. Social stressors can play a role. Lack of internal vigilance is probably more often to blame. Those who have been in recovery for some time can become overconfident or suffer from defective thinking. After being away from their substance for a considerable amount of time, addicts some-times believe that "a little won't hurt." Special situations can often be triggers—a business meeting with executives from a culture where drinking is expected, for example. All addicts, even those with a solid recovery, will come across unusual, intense temptations from time to time. However, if the addict maintains his life changes using the techniques that made him successful in becoming sober, relapse is unlikely. If relapse does occur, a fast return to sobriety is easier to achieve when the addict does not fall into shame or self-pity. If the addict has found that daily exercise or meditation has helped him to remain clean, he must continue to engage in those activities in order to guard against relapse. Working with the brain, instead of against it, helps the addict maintain his recovery. This means continually engaging in the behaviors that support recovery and excluding activities that open the door to relapse.

Termination

Termination is the end of the cycle of change. It is the state when a new lifestyle is ingrained, normal, and natural. It is a controversial stage and one that we do not use at Cliffside Malibu. Because relapse is always possible for an addict, we consider recovery to be an ongoing maintenance stage. We particularly encourage the continuing development of helping relationships, such as those found in psychotherapy. Recovery will become natural and effortless for the addict, but he must always remember that his addiction is just a few bad choices away.

Addict in Recovery: Edward Jones

Edward Jones is a superstar. In a recent poll, he had more name recognition than the President of the United States. Years ago, at only twenty-three, Edward was a star player with a professional football team that had captured the country's heart. He was on top of the world. All the best nightclubs opened their doors for him, the finest restaurants seated him immediately, and beautiful women fawned over him. Though he was always gracious, the attention embarrassed Edward.

Edward comes from humble roots. He was raised by his grandmother in rural Mississippi in a one-room house that was little more than a shack. There was no toilet, and the kitchen sink, when it worked, spurted only cold water. Edward's uncle dug the hole for the outhouse in the back when Edward moved in. As a child, Edward would stand outside, no matter what the weather, so that his grandmother could dress in private. They had no car. Clothing and shoes came from donations at the church. Bags of groceries were frequently left anonymously on their front doorstep.

When Edward was four, his mother was struck and killed by a car one evening while walking home from her job waitressing at a local diner. The accident was a hit and run, and the perpetrator was never identified. Not having his mother's killer brought to justice had a profound impact on Edward. He grew up a sad boy, a child who pined for a mother who would never return home.

One day, the middle school football coach saw Edward sitting on his grandmother's front porch looking sadly over the corn field on the opposite side of the road. He thought to himself that the boy needed something positive to do. He asked Edward if he'd like to join the football team. When Edward nodded his affirmation, the coach noticed that the boy was smiling. It was the first time he'd ever seen the child smile.

Edward found happiness on the football field where his innate athletic ability shone. He was a natural when it came to sports. Seeing potential in the child, the family's pastor convinced Edward's grandmother to allow the boy to live with a family in a nearby town so he could play for a bigger high school football program and hopefully earn a scholarship to a good college. On the football field, Edward's speed and agility far exceeded that of his opponents. But it was his incredible sense of sportsmanship that inspired the respect of his teammates, who looked to him for leadership. He was a standout in every way, even in the classroom. Diligent and hardworking, he was able to make the honor roll his senior year of high school.

Many universities courted Edward, and he was able to attend a school with an impressive football program. Though it was far from home and he hated leaving his grandmother, whom he had visited every Sunday during high school, he knew that the opportunity was of the once-in-a-lifetime variety. He didn't waste a minute of it. He excelled both on the field and off, helping lead his team to a respected bowl game victory while maintaining a 3.2 grade point average. Though two NFL teams wooed him his junior year, Edward insisted on finishing his degree.

After college, Edward was selected in the first twenty picks of the NFL draft and went to a team not too far from his grandmother. He was paid beyond anything he'd ever imagined earning as a boy. He bought his grandmother a house and himself a beautiful condo in a major city. In his first year, he played an important role in winning a critical playoff game. Edward dreamed of the Super Bowl, the Pro Bowl, and NFL glory, and he was well on his way there. Then, in a moment, everything changed.

As Edward was flying through the air to catch a touchdown pass, he was clipped by a defensive player attempting to make a tackle. It was just plain bad luck that he hit the ground the way he did. He heard the snap and felt the bone-splitting pain. He knew his career was over before he was carried even as far as the sidelines. His dreams were shattered, and that knowledge hurt worse than any injury ever could.

Fortunately, Edward had invested a good portion of the money he had earned. He was grateful that he had not lived as high on the hog as he could have, as he saw many other players do, but he still had to make adjustments to his lifestyle. He sold his expensive condo and moved to the town where he had gone to high school, only a short drive from his grandmother's house. He bought a restaurant there and settled into life after football. After all that had happened, he still considered himself lucky. He was a hometown hero and life was good for him.

But his leg hurt constantly. Even with physical therapy, he had to use a cane on occasion. Long hours spent standing at the restaurant did not help, but liquor did. Edward tried prescription painkillers, but didn't like them. They made him sleepy and his head foggy. Liquor, however, was readily available to him at work. Drinking numbed the pain in his leg to a tolerable level and made him generally gregarious and agreeable—at least at first. As Edward's drinking escalated, he went from being the laughing host to a temperamental tyrant. He began to yell at his staff. Patrons were frequently intimidated by him. Business slowed.

Realizing that he was the main reason for the business's downturn, Edward hired a manager for the restaurant. He stayed home and found he had nothing to do with his days. This only made his drinking worse because he had no reason to control himself. Edward began drinking around the clock.

It was Edward's childhood pastor who approached him about getting help. He didn't need much convincing. He was able to see and admit to himself that he had issues with alcohol. He was still young, in his late twenties, and wanted his life back. It was not the glory days of being a professional football player that Edward longed for, but the health and vigor he had enjoyed then. He was far too young, he believed, to feel as old and broken down as he did. Before the end of the week, Edward was in rehab in California.

To say that Edward was motivated would be an understatement. He arrived at the treatment center ready and willing to change. Edward was galvanized to get his life back. He wanted to be the host at his restaurant again and a man his grandmother could be proud of once more. Edward was initially overly zealous about his recovery and soon became impatient with the work. He wanted simple and easy action steps that would help him overcome his drinking for good.

Edward's biggest challenge was opening up about his feelings. He went through the motions of rehab and attended everything he was asked to, but refused to talk genuinely about his emotions. Exposing his raw emotions was just too hard, especially when it came to talking about his mother. "Just tell me what to do!" he would exclaim in frustration. "I don't need to talk. I need to do things!" After only thirty-two days in residence, Edward went back home, against his therapist's advice, feeling confident that his drinking days were behind him.

Within six weeks, Edward was back at the rehab center, thoroughly defeated. He had relapsed almost immediately upon his return home. Though he desperately wanted to be at the restaurant, he could not control his drinking when he was there. His manager had him physically put out before opening one night because Edward was so drunk and unruly that the manager feared Edward would be a danger to patrons. Being escorted out of his own place of business demoralized Edward and was the reason he returned to treatment.

This time, Edward fully participated in the program. He spoke at length about his mother and about how it felt to lose her at so young an age and never have her killer held accountable. He likened her loss to the pain he felt in his leg, a constant ache that never truly went away. The pain did not cripple him entirely, but it was ever present as was the sadness that seemed to hover over him. Once Edward made that connection, between the pain in his body and his grief over his mother's death, he had a real breakthrough. He made a decision not to be driven by his pain any longer, to look forward instead of back, and see what he had to offer the world rather than dwell in perpetual misery.

When Edward returned home, he did not go back to the restaurant full time. He still stopped in almost every day to greet customers and make them welcome, but food service was not the passion in his heart. What Edward loved was football. After conversations with his pastor and high school football coach, Edward set up a football program for rural youth. He knew that it was unlikely that any of the boys would play beyond the high school level, but he wasn't in the game to create professional players. What he wanted for the children was to give them the opportunity to grow from the sport, as he had, and to learn how to be leaders and team players, trusting others to help get a job done. He wanted the boys to learn how to collaborate and know that there was hope for them to reach their goals if they worked hard and did their best.

Though Edward's leg never got better, it stopped bothering him. Now, when it hurts him badly, he takes a low dose of an overthe-counter pain medication and sits down for a while. That is all. The pain no longer rules him. And when he thinks of his mother, he simply smiles at the memory of a woman who loved him and had the misfortune to leave him before she could know the wonderful man he knows himself to be.

7

Intervention

When family members and therapists call to inquire about our services, one of the most frequently mentioned topics is intervention. An intervention can be an important tool for helping an addict understand the need for treatment. At Cliffside Malibu, we use a particularly effective intervention model we call "loving the addict into treatment." In this type of intervention, rather than confront the addict with harsh consequences if he refuses to do as the family demands, we instead love the addict into treatment by showing him that recovery is possible, that he deserves treatment, that he is adored by his family and friends who only want the best for him, and that he really can live a better life.

Intervention Basics

"What exactly is an intervention?" is a question many people ask our intake staff. An intervention is a process designed to help an addict understand the seriousness of his condition and get him to go to treatment immediately. It is led by an interventionist, a person who keeps the family on track during the intervention and helps get the addict into treatment. Families have interventions because they are afraid for their loved one's well-being. The goal of an intervention is to help the addict become aware of his deteriorating condition and get him into treatment before additional harm is done to himself and his relationships. Interventions are a proven alternative to waiting for an addict to "hit bottom" before going to treatment. Remember, treatment can be very effective when it is done early in the addiction process. There is no need for an addict to lose everything before getting help. With an intervention, the family can safely and lovingly point out dangerous patterns to an addict before his life is completely destroyed.

Usually a family chooses to conduct an intervention when they are desperate and have tried everything they can think of to get their loved one into treatment. This is an appropriate time for an intervention. An addict who has legal trouble or heavily damaged relationships provides both the family and person running the intervention with a great deal of information that can be used to help the addict seek treatment.

Our intervention style is soft and compassionate. We use the family's and friends' deep affection for their loved one to encourage the addict into treatment. We prefer to offer a gentle hand rather than use a tough love approach. Treatment is presented to the addict as a gift; his family and friends love him and want him to be happy and have a wonderful life. There is no coercion used in this process. Family members are rarely asked to make ultimatums unless there is an immediate safety danger to the addict or his loved ones.

The principles of the stages of change are integral to our interventions. There is no force in the Stages of Change model. Rather, the therapist gently guides an addict to greater understanding of his addiction and provides the tools to change. In an intervention, the addict is gently and lovingly provided with greater understanding of his addiction by looking at himself through the eyes of his loved ones, and then he is given a resource for change—the opportunity to go to treatment.

The intervention draws its power from the gathering of loved ones. Having the right group—people whom the addict admires, loves, and respects—in the room is the key to a successful intervention. Every person involved in the intervention tells the addict why he is special, loved, and worthy of the gift of treatment. Each person also uses examples of the problems secondary to addiction—divorce, job loss, illness, etc.—to illustrate to the addict that he is living a painful and unfulfilling life. The participants then assure the addict that a better life is possible. Repetition of the information shared by each loved one reinforces these concepts and allows the addict to process the information without becoming defensive.

Loving an Addict into Treatment

There are four main goals in an intervention. First, the family and interventionist must express their desire for the addict to receive treatment. This breaks the silence around addiction and makes it an acceptable topic of conversation. Second, the addict must be motivated to go immediately into treatment. Treatment doesn't happen tomorrow or next week; it begins now. Third, once the addict is in treatment, he must be encouraged to stay in treatment for the full course of his treatment program. This is an extremely important aspect of the intervention and treatment process because many addicts begin to feel better early in treatment and leave before they have a firm foundation for long-term sobriety. However, if the family has used the intervention effectively to express their desire that he stay for the full program, he is more likely to do so. Fourth, the intervention can help prevent relapse because it motivates the family to support the addict's recovery and new, healthier lifestyle.

Loving an addict into treatment is about honoring the feelings the family has for the addict and presenting treatment as a gift. Addicts who respond well to interventions will have one or both of the following characteristics. First, they may be in the precontemplation or contemplation stage of change. They may believe that their lives cannot change and that they are beyond hope, or they may be unsure that treatment is a good option for them. Some addicts in this stage are completely unaware of their addiction. This addict needs to hear from people he still trusts that his situation requires a new and immediate plan of action. Second, addicts don't usually believe they are worthy of treatment; they don't always know how much they are loved. This can be true even for wildly successful people. Addiction so beats the addict down and demoralizes him that even if he looks good on the outside, he often feels unlovable on the inside. He needs to hear and believe that he is worth the investment of the kind of time and money treatment involves.

Loving an addict into treatment is as good for the family as it is for the addict. Family members are given an opportunity to express their feelings and, by doing so, they change their future. Regardless of whether the addict goes into treatment or not, it is as important for the family members to share their feelings as it is for the addict to hear them. Addiction causes constant feelings and expressions of frustration, anger, fear, and disappointment. In many families, the addict's problem is not spoken about openly, but in whispers behind closed doors. The type of intervention we are describing allows the family to share honestly and respectfully how addiction is affecting their lives and how painful it is to watch their loved one suffer. It is also an opportunity to express love. The family needs to express their love for the addict as surely as the addict needs to hear it. The intervention then becomes the starting point for everyone's healing.

The goal of intervention is to effect a change in the addict and the family so that negative interactions are replaced by a focus on the possibility of recovery. Loving an addict into treatment is about sharing a message of hope. It does not matter how much pain the addict has caused or how far down he has slipped physically, emotionally, or spiritually. If the addict is still breathing, he can recover.

What to Expect in an Intervention

The intervention we describe in this chapter may not look like what you have seen on television. Loving an addict into treatment differs in certain ways from more traditional interventions.

The intervention will happen very quickly after your call. Once an inquiry about an intervention has been made, we immediately make an assessment that determines whether or not an intervention is the best course of action for the particular addict being discussed. If we determine that an intervention is appropriate, the intervention team will start working with the family to plan the intervention. The goal is for the intervention to happen within less than a week of the first call; within a day or two is optimal if the family and friends can be gathered that quickly. Addiction is a critical condition that requires prompt attention. Prolonging the time between your call and the intervention has no benefit and allows more time for the addict to engage in potentially dangerous behavior.

Our intervention style takes into account the type of person the addict is and uses that information to motivate him to change. People are motivated very differently based on what they value and who they are. A professional cowboy is probably not affected by the same things as a Wall Street executive. The interventionist's first task is to learn who the addict is and what will motivate him to change. Then he must get the right people into the room for the intervention. The interventionist's role will change according to the needs of the client. Some addicts won't care about the interventionist and instead will be moved by the feelings expressed by family and friends. Other addicts will respect the interventionist as a professional and may listen to him more than their own family.

All of our interventionists are well-versed in the Stages of Change model. They understand that their role is to meet both the client and his family where they are in the stages of change. The interventionist must be flexible and have keen listening skills in order to understand the addict and help him see the hope for recovery.

Our interventions usually take place in the addict's home or an equally familiar place rather than a neutral location such as a hotel. This intervention method is about loving the addict into treatment, which means making him as comfortable as possible. We want to plant the seed of hope that recovery is literally waiting for him just outside his line of sight. If an intervention is conducted in a person's home with the people he loves, the addict will feel less defensive or combative than if the intervention were held elsewhere. The goal is to create a feeling of safety and connection in the comfort of home.

When the addict leaves for treatment, his family members have the potential to begin their own healing. They are together to give one another support during this emotionally intense time. Follow-up therapeutic services are suggested for the family. Do not expect the addict to go away to treatment and come back with a solution to all the family's problems. For the addict to stay sober, the family's entire dynamic must change. Just as every family member played a part in creating the conditions in which the addict could remain unhealthy, now everyone must work together to create a new, healthier environment. The intervention is like the leap from a starting block at the beginning of a lap swim; it is only the beginning, but the beginning of something with tremendous benefits.

How to Schedule an Intervention

To schedule an intervention, begin by calling the treatment center you are considering and ask if they conduct interventions. Ask what style of intervention they use. Make sure that you are comfortable with the interventionist and his plan, the timeline, and the costs before agreeing to an intervention from any provider.

When an inquiry is made to our center, the Cliffside Malibu intervention team immediately begins an assessment to determine whether or not an intervention will be a useful tool for the addict in question. In making the assessment, the team must ask some important questions. Is the addict in the precontemplation or contemplation stage of change? If either is the case, the addict is a good candidate for intervention.

Can the family get the right group—people whom the addict trusts and loves—to the intervention? Are these people available and willing to participate and share their feelings in a genuine and loving way? The intervention is not a time for finger-pointing and blame, but rather an opportunity for the family to express the love they have for the addict. Everyone in the room must be capable of this kind of expression. These are only a few of the many issues that are considered when assessing whether or not an intervention is the best course of action.

Once an assessment has been made, the interventionist meets the family to help them prepare for the intervention. The interventionist's goal is to get a better sense of family dynamics and build the family's confidence so that they can confront the addict lovingly. He teaches the family how to express their feelings and frustrations in a way that says to the addict, "I want you to see how wonderful you really are and how worthy you are of receiving the gift of treatment." Families are emotionally charged units. The interventionist will coach the family so that they will also receive the full benefits of the intervention and understand the message of hope that recovery, living a healthier life, is possible for all of them.

After the intervention, follow-up is done with the family. The intervention team must ensure that the family will do what it takes to provide a safe and secure environment for the addict to return to after treatment. Follow-up also includes providing support for the family members and making them aware of the professional resources that are available to help them to improve their own lives. Intervention follow-up reminds families that everyone can benefit from a healthier lifestyle if they are willing to make a commitment to change and do the work to achieve it.

Addict in Recovery: George Wilson

George Wilson had a charmed life. As a forty-eight-year-old senior executive at a major US manufacturing firm, he had few concerns. Yes, he had a great deal of responsibility at work, but he treasured the time he spent with his wife and two teenage daughters. George owned a large house on which he had no mortgage, and he kept a small fishing boat at a marina an hour from his home. He planned to retire at the age of fifty-five, only a short time away. George was handsome and enjoyed solid relationships at work and with family friends. His was not at all the picture that comes to mind when one thinks of an addict.

George was always the type of person who made overachievers look lazy. He went to Brown and then Stanford. As an undergraduate, he was a member of a fraternity and drank hard, but not so much that it ever got in the way of his studies. In business school he started using cocaine. It helped him to stay focused, something he sometimes found difficult, especially when faced with enormous, complicated school projects. After earning his MBA, he took a job as a junior executive with a large company. Under pressure to prove himself to his new employers, he continued to use cocaine, if only on occasion, as a sort of supplement to help him work late. As he climbed the corporate ladder, he found that his drug use increased from a few times a month to a few times a week to every day. By the time George was forty-five, he could not get out of bed without snorting a line of coke.

As his drug use escalated, George tried to minimize his interactions with others so as not to damage his relationships. He focused entirely on work, where his performance was slipping despite his long hours. Though he tried to hide his drug use from his family, his wife became aware of his habit, and his children were increasingly horrified by their father's unpredictable and erratic behavior. After achieving so much professionally and personally, George was on the verge of losing it all.

"Am I really an addict?" George asked the interventionist his family called. His tone was one of incredulity and utter disbelief. His family was shocked by his denial. A week earlier, at a high school graduation party for his eldest daughter, George had, without provocation, flown off the handle at a guest and in a rage smashed a chair to bits on the stone fireplace. Four weeks earlier, George had been hospitalized with chest pain. The doctor had warned George that his drug use might trigger a heart attack, but George dismissed the warning as "overprotective nonsense" and continued as before. George's wife and daughters, fed up with his foul moods and bad behavior, decided to stage an intervention, one last stand as a family before the eldest girl went to college.

George agreed to go to treatment primarily because the treatment center was luxurious. He imagined he was going away to a spa for a few weeks. His family was just happy that he was going away.

George stayed ten weeks in treatment, not because he liked the massages and gourmet food, which he did enjoy, but because he found, for the first time in his life, that he could stop running from the pain that had pushed him since his childhood.

George shared with his therapist that he drove himself as hard as he did because he had been largely ignored by his impoverished parents. George's father was a drunk, and a mean one at that. Overachieving was George's way of keeping the peace in his household and proving to his father that he had value. When his father would begin to rage about how expensive it was to have a child, George would show his father his latest report card or the project he was working on for the science fair. These achievements pacified George's father and often kept George and his mother from being beaten. When George was perceived by his father as an achiever, he was valued as something more than just another mouth to feed. Over time, George formed the belief that he had no value outside his work and took that conviction with him throughout his life. A pattern developed; in order to feel validated, George set impossible goals and used cocaine to help attain them. Eventually, he became addicted. Fortunately, George's wife and daughters helped him find treatment before every aspect of his life, including his work and health, were destroyed.

Once George was helped to see the truth that he was an addict, he had no trouble at all following the regimen that would help him recover. In conversations with his wife, while in treatment, George decided that part of his sobriety action plan would be to leave his high stress corporate job when his youngest daughter finished high school. He had enough money set aside for his daughters to attend state universities. Meanwhile, George laid the groundwork to start his own business. After both girls were in college, George and his wife sold their home and moved to the lakeside community where George kept his boat. Together, they established a small inn in a renovated historic home and shared inn-keeping duties. George also started taking people out on the lake to fish and selling handmade fishing poles to local anglers.

"After I learned what was driving my addiction," says George, "all desire to use cocaine anymore was gone. I want to spend the years I have left with my family, not as a slave to my father's fears and worries. I couldn't be more grateful to the people who introduced me to the stages of change and helped me find a life I am passionate about living. Having the inn with my wife, making and selling fishing poles, spending time with my daughters, this really is the stuff dreams are made of!"

8

The Cliffside Malibu Treatment Protocol

When we decided to write this book, many people asked why we would share the secret of an addiction treatment protocol as successful as ours, seven times more effective than twelve-step programs alone. Wouldn't it be in our interest to keep the secrets of our success to ourselves? No. The fact is that we are both addicts and have seen far too much suffering among addicts and their families. We want others to recover to lead the lives they've always dreamed of. It is our sincerest hope in discussing exactly how we treat people at Cliffside Malibu that we will move the entire addiction treatment industry forward. We want people to know that they really can recover from addiction, and we will share every part of the life-changing treatment we provide.

In truth, it is our experience that getting sober without the benefit of quality treatment is difficult. Addicts flourish in a supportive, compassionate treatment environment with a variety of services. In one day at Cliffside Malibu, a client might receive the services of ten or more professionals, from therapists to personal trainers, acupuncturists, massage therapists, psychiatrists, personal physicians, and other trained professionals as needed or desired. Can an individual realistically coordinate all those services on his own for an extended period of time so that he creates positive habits? Chances are not good. Thus, we encourage treatment for those who need it, whether it is with us or elsewhere. However, if a treatment facility is absolutely out of the question, the following are the most-often used types of support services at Cliffside Malibu. This list will give you a starting point for creating your own comprehensive recovery program.

The Mind

The problem of addiction rests most solidly in the mind. Addiction has physical and spiritual components and repercussions, but the root of behavioral disorders is in the psyche. Advances in neuroscience have taught us that addiction is primarily a brain disorder, in which the brain changes its function and structure so that the addict can no longer make positive, healthy choices. In order to effectively "rewire" the brain to create the opportunity for healthy decision making, the addict requires extensive, intensive one-on-one psychotherapy.

Addicts think differently than non-addicts. This is true regardless of the drug of choice or the pattern of behavior. Only addicts think, though they may not be able to admit it to themselves, "Drinking every night of the week until I vomit is a great way to deal with life's problems," or, "If two pain pills help with the pain from this dental procedure, four will be even better." This distorted thinking is a function of changes to the addict's brain. Consequently, in regular, intensive one-on-one therapy, the addict will discover the reasons why he abuses substances, find the willingness to make changes, and then develop an action plan for creating a lasting, sober life-style. This work will help to change the way the brain works, freeing the addict from addictive behavior patterns.

Styles of Psychotherapy

There are hundreds of different types of psychotherapy, most of which can be categorized into particular schools of thought. Some of the major schools are psychoanalytic, psychodynamic, experiential, existential, interpersonal, cognitive, behavioral, exposure, and eclectic. Each of these schools of psychotherapy has a particular way of explaining why people have problems and specific methods to address those problems. Though graduate psychology programs have a specific focus, licensed therapists will all have a basic understanding of each of these types of therapy. Whether a therapist received his training in Jungian psychology, gestalt therapy, or a cognitive-behavioral school, he will still be aware of the other approaches to psychotherapy and may choose to incorporate some ideas, concepts, or activities from those other schools into his practice.

Because intensive psychotherapy makes up the core of the treatment protocol here, we employ many psychotherapists who have a diverse array of backgrounds, experiences, and training. We do this for a number of reasons. First, we ensure that no therapist is ever seeing more than four residents at a time. In this way, we can guarantee that our therapists are available to clients regularly. The therapist is able to provide solid and consistent support in the recovery process because he has the time to concentrate on each client. Second, we are committed to matching addicts with a therapist with whom they can create a strong therapeutic relationship. To do this, we need to be able to choose from different types of people with different types of training and ways of conducting therapy. Third, we employ therapists who might be trained in a particular school of therapeutic thought, but who can also borrow from other schools if that is what the client needs. This is how we take a transtheoretical approach to psychotherapy.

There is no single psychotherapeutic school that is the most effective at relieving suffering for all clients. Therefore, our therapists determine where the addict is in the stages of change and, based on conversations with the client and other professionals, take the approach to change they feel will best serve the client. In some cases, this may mean providing treatment closely in line with a particular type of psychology. Just as often, it will mean borrowing treatment approaches from different schools as the client's needs change and he becomes increasingly comfortable in his sober life. In every case, the client's needs and preferences are central to determining which therapeutic approaches to take.

Approach and Content:
Meeting People Where They Are

The Stages of Change theory is rooted in the transtheoretical view of psychology. It teaches the therapist to learn who his client really is and why he is hurting. The psychologist must help the client examine his beliefs about himself and understand how he operates in the world. Then, in discussion, the therapist must provide the client with the tools that are most likely to help him believe that change is possible and that he can create a new and better life. If the client isn't interested in dream analysis or doesn't have the requisite attention to write journal entries or completely rejects the notion of twelve-step programs, a therapist must not use those tools no matter what that therapist's area of expertise may be. Change occurs when the client believes it can occur. We encourage all therapists to tailor their psychological tools to each client's needs. This personalization of each individual therapy program is what makes our clients so successful at recovering from addiction for good.

Co-occurring Disorders

An addict with a co-occurring disorder suffers from addiction and another mental disorder. Co-occurring disorders usually refer to problems that are related. Addiction and gout, for example, might appear in the same person, but this does not meet the definition of a co-occurring disorder as we are using the term. Co-occurring disorders in an addiction treatment context refer to other forms of mental illness including, but not limited to, clinical depression, anxiety disorders, and post-traumatic stress disorder (PTSD). Another term applied to those with co-occurring disorders is "dual diagnosis patients."

Those with co-occurring mental disorders require special treatment. People with mental illness often use drugs and alcohol to self-medicate and mask their symptoms. Substances can also worsen the symptoms of mental illness, thereby exacerbating depression and anxiety and making social interactions even more difficult than they would be otherwise. In fact, drugs and alcohol can actually trigger mental illness. For example, long-term abuse of cocaine can cause anxiety

and panic attacks. Some medications used to treat mental illness can have dangerous interactions with alcohol, street drugs, and other prescribed medicine. A psychiatrist specially trained in addiction recovery can provide the specific treatment needed in each case.

Co-occurring disorders are extremely common in addiction recovery. It is estimated that somewhere between 25 and 50 percent of those with mental illness also have a problem with addiction. The connection is logical. A war veteran who has served four tours in Iraq and Afghanistan and returns home with PTSD is highly likely to medicate himself with alcohol or other drugs in order to avoid horrible and painful feelings. A woman suffering from post-partum depression after the birth of her first child could find that taking drugs makes her sadness go away, and she can take better care of her baby. A cocaine addict who has been using for seven years and has a history of mental illness may find that after a period of sobriety, his anxiety and paranoia, thought to be drug induced, do not diminish. All of these people will benefit from specialized treatment for addiction and their co-occurring mental illness. For these addicts, the prognosis is optimistic. They can recover from addiction just as well as an addict without a co-occurring disorder. They simply need specialized treatment, extra attention, and support.

EMDR
(Eye Movement Desensitization and Reprocessing)

One of the more common approaches to the treatment of co-occurring disorders, particularly PTSD, is eye movement desensitization and reprocessing (EMDR).

EMDR is a psychotherapy technique that combines talk therapy with bilateral eye movement in order to change the brain's relationship to troubling memories. It has been shown in clinical studies to be successful in helping those who suffer from trauma, particularly PTSD, though how the combination of eye movement and talk therapy helps people overcome severe trauma remains uncertain. Before EMDR, mental illnesses such as PTSD were very difficult to treat and required long-term care. EMDR, however, has been proven to foster tremendous healing in short periods of time, bringing lasting relief to those suffering from severe emotional distress.

How does EMDR work? It was once widely believed that severe emotional trauma, such as childhood sexual abuse or war-related memories, took a long time and great effort to heal. EMDR changed that belief. In the body, once an irritant is removed, healing will occur. When you get a splinter in your finger, for example, you need to remove it in order for the wound to heal. If you leave the splinter in place, the wound will fester and might become infected. EMDR works on the same principle; if mental health is blocked by the continued remembrance of a particular event in a way that causes the patient pain, EMDR is used to remove that block just as you might use tweezers to remove a splinter from a finger. Once the block is removed, the client changes his relationship to the past event, and sees it no longer as a source of pain, but often as a source of strength. In this way, the psyche mirrors the natural healing processes used by the physical body. While it is unclear exactly how EMDR works on the brain's neurobiology, it has been shown conclusively to have a positive effect on the relationship one has to disturbing memories.

Combined with other forms of therapy used in addiction treatment, EMDR can be a useful tool in treating those with addiction and some co-occurring disorders. EMDR is one of many treatments available to those who need specialized support for their psychological well-being.

The Body

Most addicts neglect their bodies. Drug addicts and alcoholics generally don't eat regularly or well. They rarely exercise. They ignore the recommended dosage on medications. Drug abuse leads to many physical problems. Many drugs, if taken in high doses or for long periods, can cause brain damage. Intravenous drug use can lead to infections and the spread of disease. Taking too much of a drug may cause an overdose leading to respiratory distress, heart failure, and/or death. It is rare to find an addict in treatment who does not suffer from at least a small number of physical problems.

Detox

Detox is a supervised, controlled withdrawal from drugs and alcohol. In order for the addict to engage fully in the psychological change processes of addiction treatment, he must first be free from the substances he abuses. Detox is supervised because, depending on the substance(s) used, amount used, and length of use, the addict's withdrawal from the drug(s) he abuses can have serious physical consequences, sometimes including death. Qualified personnel should always supervise an addict's detox so that complications may be addressed and treated as they occur.

We believe in making detox as comfortable for the addict as possible. We find the practice of letting the addict experience the full misery of detox so that he won't forget it, abjectly cruel. Detox is not a punishment; it is a biological process of removing toxins from the system. We view detox as a biological issue and treat it without judgment. A client's personal physician uses all available tools to diminish the worst of a client's withdrawal symptoms. These symptoms can include vomiting, nausea, constipation or diarrhea, severe agitation, muscle aches and flu-like symptoms, severe anxiety, and hot or cold flashes. More severe withdrawal symptoms can include seizures, psychotic breaks, and heart failure. The type and duration of withdrawal symptoms a patient might experience depend on his overall health, the types of substances he used, the length of time he used, and the amount he used. Some drugs are short acting, meaning that withdrawal symptoms will last for perhaps a few days to a week. Other drugs are longer acting, requiring longer detoxification periods.

Detoxification alone is in no way an addiction cure. Many well-meaning family and friends think, "If we can just get the drugs out of his system, he'll be okay." This is a fallacy. Detox is only the process of separating the physical body from the abused substances and, while detox is necessary for recovery, it does nothing to address the reasons why the addict abused substances in the first place. Those who receive only detox support and no other treatment will almost inevitably return to substance abuse, usually in the short term. Detox support should be viewed as a precursor to extended addiction treatment.

Fitness

Fitness is defined as a person's overall level of physical health as measured by cardiovascular endurance, muscle strength and endurance, flexibility, and overall leanness of body composition. Fitness is achieved through exercise, a combination of cardiovascular training, strength training, and stretching. Regular exercise, even mild exercise, can improve health, appearance, and self-esteem.

Exercise is especially important for recovering addicts because it provides the natural chemicals needed to restore mental and emotional well-being. When addicts use, the pleasure centers of the brain are flooded with chemicals, some of which are natural to the body. For example, when a person uses cocaine, dopamine levels increase to two or three times their normal levels. This feels great! When the high wears off, dopamine levels can drop to far below normal. This feels terrible and the addict uses again to recapture the high. There is no doubt drugs affect brain chemistry. In the short term, after detox is complete, the addict's brain chemistry frequently remains imbalanced. Production of natural feel-good chemicals, like dopamine, may be suppressed. However, exercise releases these chemicals and restores a feeling of well-being to the addict, thereby uplifting his mind, spirit, and body.

Nutrition

Proper nutrition goes hand in hand with exercise and leading a balanced lifestyle. Good nutrition means providing the body with the appropriate calories, minerals, vitamins, and other nutrients it needs to be healthy. Addicts rarely eat well when using. They either don't eat regularly or they eat junk food, which is no different than putting cheap fuel into a fine race car. The car might run, but it will sputter and perform poorly.

Maintaining a balanced diet and a healthy weight is just as important for the addict as it is for anyone else. It will give him vitality and energy, boost his immune system, delay the effects of aging, allow for an active lifestyle, diminish fatigue, improve concentration and mood, and even potentially ward off or reverse serious medical concerns such as type 2 diabetes, heart disease, high blood pressure, and certain cancers. Diets should provide adequate calories for a person's age and body type, be high in fiber, contain fresh fruits and vegetables, and limit fat and highly processed foods.

Orthomolecular Therapies

Sometimes, to create and maintain health, good nutrition and exercise are not enough. Addicts can reach treatment in such poor physical health that nutritional supplements are required to bring the body's systems into balance. Cliffside Malibu provides orthomolecular therapy to clients who require more physical support than just diet and exercise.

Orthomolecular therapy means "correct molecules." It is the process of using the proper substances to bring health to the body. The term was coined by molecular biologist and two-time Nobel Prize winner Linus Pauling. Orthomolecular medicine seeks to prevent and treat disease by giving the body optimal amounts of the natural substances it lacks. It is based on an understanding of health as a balanced biochemical state in the body. It uses only natural substances—vitamins, minerals, fatty acids, amino acids, and trace elements—to adjust the body's chemistry. Orthomolecular therapy supplements a nutritious diet in order to accelerate the body's return to health after suffering from neglect and addiction. Research has also shown that in addition to psychotherapy and more traditional psychiatric interventions, orthomolecular therapy diminishes the symptoms of those suffering from depression, anxiety, and other mental disorders. It can also support healing among those with specific biomedical diseases such as certain types of cancer and atherosclerosis.

Massage

The skin, our largest organ, functions as a barrier between our internal body and the external environment. Through touch, the skin provides sensory perception. The skin is a vital and important part of the body and must be cared for.

Massage is the pressing, rubbing, and general manipulation of skin and muscle for therapeutic benefit. Massage therapists typically use their hands and forearms to do their work, but may also use their elbows and, in some forms of massage, feet. The touch used in massage can range from light to deep pressure. Massage is not just available in spas; it has many health benefits and is now widely used as a complementary health practice in a variety of facilities from airports to hospitals.

The healing touch of bodywork calms the nerves and removes negative and irritating energies. Healthy and nurturing massage can help facilitate difficult emotional processes and ease worries and fears. Sometimes massage therapy will allow the client to acknowledge and release painful memories and blockages. Being able to experience the calm that results from the therapist's caring attention to the body accelerates the process of healing. When emotional barriers are removed, the body finds its own balance.

Studies have shown that massage has many benefits such as reducing stress, relieving pain and muscle stiffness, moving lymph, managing depression and anxiety, and boosting immunity. Massage can also be particularly healing for people who have had their personal boundaries violated through physical or sexual abuse. Massage can give these individuals a sense of empowerment and control over their bodies. Many enjoy massage purely for the comfort it brings and the relationship that is developed between the client and the massage therapist.

Acupuncture

Acupuncture is a holistic healing modality that has been used in China and much of East Asia for thousands of years. The acupuncturist's work is based on the idea that body, mind, and spirit are connected in ways that are often beyond our understanding. To heal, the whole of the individual must be brought into balance. Acupuncture is more concerned with the causes of disease and energetic imbalance than with treating symptoms, although acupuncturists do offer treatments to relieve the symptoms of a variety of conditions.

To promote harmony and healing, acupuncturists place very thin needles into the skin along points on twelve meridians. Each of these meridians, or energy channels, is a circuit along which qi flows. Qi (pronounced chee) is the life force or energy that animates all living beings. When qi is blocked or imbalanced, the individual becomes ill. By placing needles into the body, qi is redirected, promoting healing. Acupuncture has been shown to be highly effective in treating an array of physical and psychological problems.

There is an acupuncture protocol specific to addiction treatment. The NADA protocol, which was created by the National Acupuncture Detoxification Association, is a specific treatment designed to relax addicts and ease withdrawal symptoms. Addicts treated with this protocol report feeling energized and less stressed after a treatment. Acupuncture in early sobriety can reduce anxiety and promote sleep. Studies have even reported that those treated with this protocol are more optimistic about treatment and recovery and are more likely to stay in treatment than those who do not receive acupuncture.

Acupuncture is an extremely important tool in addiction recovery. It can be used as an adjunct to psychotherapy and a support to many interventions that need to be made.

Other Resources

In addition to the treatments discussed above, Cliffside Malibu offers supplemental treatments for those who need them. These resources include brain mapping and hyperbaric oxygen therapy among others, and they are used on a highly individualized basis, only by those who need the additional support. We share them here in the event that they are available in your area, and you or the one you love would benefit from them.

Brain mapping relates the brain's function to its structure. We know that certain areas of the brain are in control of certain tasks from breathing to speech to impulse control. Because drugs can damage the brain, there are times when residents require brain scans, which are then related to brain maps. These scans allow the client's personal physician to work in conjunction with our therapists and staff to understand whether or not some abilities are compromised due to cerebral dysfunction or damage. We can use this information to optimize recovery even if there has been some irreparable damage to the brain itself.

Clients with evident organic damage to the brain will be given the opportunity to receive hyperbaric chamber treatments. Hyperbaric Oxygen Therapy (HBOT) is the use of high-pressure oxygen in a specialized environment. Though initially used to treat decompression sickness and air embolisms, HBOT has shown success in the treatment of traumatic brain injury and brain damage caused by long-term alcohol abuse. While studies are ongoing, initial reports indicate that HBOT does accelerate brain recovery in brain-damaged individuals when used in conjunction with other therapies.

The Spirit

The spiritual aspect of addiction recovery is the most objectionable to addicts and the most controversial among addiction recovery professionals. What do we mean by spiritual healing and who is qualified to assist the addict in his healing process?

At Cliffside Malibu, we define the term spirit loosely and do not infuse it with any religious connotation. When we refer to the spirit, we mean that sense of joy and enthusiasm for life that we want to help all addicts experience. We are talking about hope and the belief that a meaningful future can be envisioned and achieved. With this framework in mind, we help addicts find a variety of opportunities for spiritual development and for building and expanding their concept of hope for the future. We do this by providing access to professionals who can guide an addict in methods of nonreligious spiritual development. Opportunities to speak with clergy of any tradition can also be accommodated as requested. This area of development is particularly important in an addict's aftercare plan and is often set up using existing relationships in the addict's community.

Yoga and Meditation

While yoga is a form of exercise that stretches the muscles and promotes balance, it can also be a positive tool for spiritual growth. In combination with meditation, the practice of quieting the mind and calming the spirit, it can be a powerful tool for addiction recovery.

Today, there is a broad understanding of the full spectrum of yoga's value and its powerful transformative psychological, mental, emotional, and physical health benefits. The most immediate effect of yoga practice is developing a state of mindfulness. This is the state that occurs while concentrating on the breath during yoga poses or meditation. Mindfulness is a nonjudgmental attention to the present moment. The breath is the bridge between the body and the mind. When we focus on the rhythmic nature of breathing, we become mindful because we are acutely aware of the present. Mindfulness promotes a sense of calm and the appreciation that at this very instant all is well. Profound healing can take place during the practice of mindful breathing. Mindfulness has been studied extensively, in particular by Dr. Dan Siegel of UCLA and the Mindsight Institute. The evidence of the relationship between mindfulness and brain change is profound.

In yoga, we do not judge ourselves or anyone else. It doesn't matter if we do the poses well or even at all. The practitioner is gently urged to notice what he can and cannot do without getting emotional about his perceived success or failure. This is another form of mindfulness, noticing what is happening without judgment. While practicing mindfulness, we become aware of our own thoughts, emotions, and sensations without evaluating them. The practice of yoga can teach addicts how not to sweat the small stuff and how to refrain from making judgments that serve no positive purpose.

A fulfilling yoga and/or meditation practice is grounded in non-judgment. This is an incredibly important lesson for addicts to learn. Addicts constantly berate themselves for the slightest mistakes or imperfections and often criticize themselves even when they've done nothing wrong. Yoga and meditation cultivate self-forgiveness. You can't come close to getting into a particular posture? It doesn't matter. We all do the best we can in the moment. As the addict practices yoga and meditation, this principle takes hold. He becomes gentler with himself and kinder to others.

Meditation can be part of a yoga practice or done on its own. It is the act of quietly noticing what is going on in the mind, watching that information pass without judgment, and learning to become more centered in the moment. Meditation does not have to be done perfectly or even well to have benefits. When practiced in conjunction with yoga, meditation can support a healthier lifestyle by helping the individual slow down and make better choices; be used as a tool to cope with depression, anxiety, fear, anger, trauma, and other negative emotions; instill a sense of calm even during challenging moments by releasing stress from the organs and central nervous system; aid in the development of positive behaviors leading to greater self-control; and improve body image by making one more at peace with one's self.

Twelve-Step Programs

Twelve-step programs are perhaps the most controversial aspect of addiction treatment. Some treatment centers use the twelve-steps as the core of their treatment protocol while other centers don't use these principles at all. Similarly, addicts respond in different ways to twelve-step programs. Some are very motivated by the program, particularly the camaraderie and community developed through participating in twelve-step meetings. Others want nothing to do with the program.

What are twelve-step programs? Twelve-step programs are self-help groups that are based on Alcoholics Anonymous (AA). AA was conceived in 1935 in Akron, Ohio, when two alcoholics got together to help one another stay sober. AA's membership is voluntary. Its purpose is to help members stay sober and help those who are struggling to achieve sobriety. Early members of the group developed a twelve-step treatment program that focuses on character and spiritual development. This program is detailed in *The Big Book*, AA's basic text and the book used by most twelve-step programs.

The program of recovery suggests reliance on a higher power, which can be the god of a particular religious tradition or any concept outside the addict; the idea is that the addict is not God or in control of his future. The program teaches powerlessness over addiction and asks that the addict set right past wrongs in whatever ways are possible while working to improve the addict's interpersonal relations and teaching him how to interact with others more effectively. There are prayer and meditation components to the program that are optional. Mutual support is given through attendance at meetings and a relationship with a sponsor, another addict who shares his experience with the newer addict.

We introduce all addicts to the concept of the twelve-steps and encourage everyone to attend at least one twelve-step meeting just to see what it is all about. Twelve-step programs have helped millions of people become sober and maintain their sobriety over the past seventy-plus years. Twelve-step meetings can be found in almost any city or town in the United States and in many places worldwide. Accessing this network of addicts in recovery can help an addict if he finds himself having difficulty at any time of the day or night and in almost any place in the world. For those who do not have a strong support network at home, twelve-step programs can be a place for addicts to find the support they need. There are many benefits to participation in a twelve-step program. We believe it is important to give all residents an introduction to what the twelve steps have to offer.

However, we are not a twelve-step-based recovery facility, nor do we consider twelve-step work "treatment." We view twelve-step work as an adjunct to our treatment program, a supplement that encourages and supports sobriety, particularly once the addict returns home.

Spiritual Counseling

As noted in several places throughout this book, the spiritual aspect of each human being cannot be ignored if treatment is to be successful. The way in which one chooses to express his spiritual side, however, is inconsequential to recovery. The addict must find a path to spiritual growth that feels good to him. He might find his spirituality through a particular religious practice or through spending time in nature. Before treatment, spiritual development is usually impossible. It is difficult to develop any type of spirituality when an addict is consistently damaging himself with drugs and alcohol.

Our spiritual counselors serve as guides to help addicts unearth the spiritual practices that work best for them based on their interests and needs. These practices could include prayer, meditation, attendance at twelve-step meetings or religious services, or other spiritual rituals. Concepts such as values, ideas about right and wrong, and the spirit's intuitive ability to direct and heal are discussed. Our goal is to help each resident find comfort and wholeness in a spiritual practice that is familiar and inspiring.

Clients who belong to a particular religious tradition are encouraged to speak with a member of the clergy of their faith. Clergy who have had an ongoing relationship before treatment with an addict can be particularly helpful in encouraging an individual to change. Many houses of worship offer support specific to addicts. Ask how your member of the clergy can help you.

RICHARD TAITE & CONSTANCE SCHARFF

Addict in Recovery: Alicia Manning

Alicia Manning is the daughter of an A-list movie star and was the poster child for over-indulged youth gone wild. Three years ago, at just twenty-four, she had already been in rehab three times. She'd also been arrested for possession of an illegal substance and driving under the influence and had numerous humiliating photographs splashed across the tabloids. She was beautiful and she was out of control. Resigned to her path of self-destruction, she expected to become part of the infamous 27 Club, a group of celebrities that have all died at the age of 27. The only future Alicia imagined for herself was as a corpse.

From the outside looking in, it would be hard to imagine how a young woman who grew up as privileged as Alicia had could be so entirely lost. Just below the surface, the reasons become clearer. Alicia's father is a three-time Academy Award nominee and one time Oscar winner whose image has graced billboards and magazine covers for more than three decades. He is in every way a superstar. But if you're his daughter, he's also an embarrassment. Alicia's father is well-known in Hollywood for his philandering, especially with the youngest up-and-coming actresses. Although Alicia is his only child, he never paid attention to her. He was always much more interested in what Alicia called his "starlet of the moment." No matter what Alicia tried to do to get his attention, she could never hold it. Instead of blaming him for his lack of interest in her, Alicia turned her anger inward, wondering what was wrong with her that her father could not love her.

At about fifteen, when Alicia realized that she would not win her father's love by being good, she decided to be bad. She began using meth regularly. She liked it because it kept her thin and made it easy to party all night. She also took Ecstasy. It lowered her inhibitions and allowed her to sleep with the worst kinds of men, men her father would hate, who took advantage of her and forced her to perform sexual acts she wasn't comfortable with. She took painkillers too because when the men she was with beat and demeaned her, she needed some way to numb herself. And, of course, she drank. Alicia started every day off with two long pulls from a vodka bottle she kept underneath her bed. She was the kind of addict who had no true drug of choice, but rather used anything and everything she could get her hands on.

Alicia's goal was singular; she wanted to be the greatest shame possible to her father before she overdosed and died. If you asked her why she behaved as she did, she was rational enough to say just that. To her therapist and friends, this level of anger and spitefulness was shocking. Alicia was too beautiful and intelligent a woman, they believed, to destroy herself as an act of revenge, yet that is precisely what Alicia hoped to do.

Intervention, for Alicia, happened in the form of a car accident. In a drunken stupor, she ran her Mercedes off Pacific Coast Highway straight into and through the door of her neighbor's garage. The property damage was significant. So, too, were Alicia's injuries, which landed her in the hospital. Alicia's mother sat weeping beside her daughter's bed while Alicia lay handcuffed. "I don't know what to do to make the pain go away," Alicia's mother whispered, kissing her daughter's forehead, "but I don't want you to die. I love you. I wish my love alone was enough to make you better."

Although not convinced that Alicia had any hope of recovery, the judge who sentenced her for driving under the influence was persuaded that a private treatment facility paid for by Alicia's family was a better alternative than jail paid for by the state. Thus, the judge ordered that Alicia was to receive no less than ninety days of addiction treatment in an in-patient facility to be approved by the court. Failure to complete this treatment without incident would result in jail time. Alicia accepted the verdict, preferring the idea of a luxury treatment facility to incarceration.

Instead of viewing treatment as a gift, Alicia saw it as a punishment to be tolerated. She was aggressive and argumentative with the treatment center's staff and reclusive when approached by other residents. She liked to spend her time alone in her room. However, despite her efforts to disengage, Alicia found herself drawn to a lovely, motherly woman from Vermont, Amy Green, who had entered treatment only a week before she had. When they met, Amy immediately saw in Alicia the hurt child beneath the façade she put up and befriended her. Alicia, after her detox, sorely needed someone parental. A heartfelt connection was made between the women.

Though the relationship could have been twisted by each woman's neediness, the connection between Amy and Alicia was healthy. They sat together at dinner and shared with each other the trials and triumphs of their days. They did one another's nails. They stayed up late, talking about their disappointments with their families—Amy about the sadness she felt when her children left home and finding out so late in life that she was adopted, and Alicia about what it felt like to be just another of her father's adoring fans, loving him intensely, but receiving nothing in return. They discussed what it must be like for Alicia's mother to watch her daughter slowly kill herself, feeling all the while as if her attention and love were not enough to fill the void left by Alicia's father.

Prior to the development of the friendship between Alicia and Amy, Alicia was the most difficult kind of addict to treat. She knew she was an addict but had no interest in changing. She wanted to die rather than build a life for herself. Once she was befriended by Amy, however, Alicia was able to open herself up to the love and support that was already in her life. Through the haze of drugs and anger toward her father, Alicia had been unable to feel her mother's love for her. She didn't realize that she had other family support and several solid, steadfast friends. Amy was able to help Alicia broaden her world view so that it included images, ideas, hopes, and aspirations beyond her father.

Working with her therapist, Alicia eventually developed a sense of compassion for her father. She realized that his life was empty—that he had fame and fortune, but no real connection to anyone and no true experience of love. Alicia began to see her father more completely as a hollow man who filled his emptiness with the applause of adoring fans. His attention, if he was capable of giving it, would not be much comfort to her. He certainly was not worth dying for.

After her treatment was complete, Alicia returned home where she stayed until her next court date. The judge was impressed with her changed demeanor and humble expression of remorse for her crime. She has not been in trouble with the law again.

While in treatment, Alicia was particularly focused on her goals for the future and decided to start her own business, something that would draw on her love of fashion. She enrolled in a world-renowned design school where instructors and students were surprised and pleased to find Alicia a talented designer and a hard worker. She used her family's personal connections to gain access to an impressive internship opportunity. Alicia now sells high-end handbags at boutiques in New York, Los Angeles, London, and Milan. She is in the process of expanding her business to include a shoe line.

Alicia and Amy remain friends.

9

A Message of Hope

Every day addicts recover from a desperate disorder. Families are repaired. Lives are rebuilt. Hope is restored. The addict you love can also recover, if he is willing to get help.

The healing we do at Cliffside Malibu continues to inspire us. Families call us on the phone or e-mail us distressed and hopeless. Addicts come through our doors demoralized and sick. Then, through a process of collaboration that requires courage, determination, and faith, hopelessness slips away. By the time the addict leaves treatment, he is already starting to experience joy and possibility. He is reunited with his family and they marvel at the return of his optimism and interest in life. The issues of the past have been largely resolved and a new, good life beyond the addict's wildest imagining is no longer an aspiration, but a reality.

Cliffside Malibu was built on the premise that the best care possible should be given to addicts. In the years since its inception, the facility has been a place for the application of the most cutting edge addiction treatments available. We have developed a treatment protocol that is truly synergistic, providing more than the sum of its parts. Each treatment activity works in harmony with the others to support and heal the addict holistically on the levels of mind, body, and spirit.

If you have read this book, you or the addict you love may be in dire circumstances. Addiction may have ripped your world apart. The addict in your life may not know he has a problem or could be so deeply demoralized that he does not believe there is hope for him. He might be too afraid of judgment or failure to take action or he may believe that he's just not worth the time and effort. Addicts don't see the world the way other people do; they believe in the worst because they have experienced the worst. They no longer believe they are capable of living a fulfilling life.

We understand how the addict thinks because we understand the nature of addiction. Treating addiction as a behavioral disorder, our deeply committed professionals lead addicts through a process of change that works to establish the addict's sober lifestyle and make long-term recovery possible. We know that the idea of transitioning from a life confined by addiction to the freedom of sobriety seems daunting, even overwhelming, but with baby steps and the help of a quality treatment team, change is possible. How do we know? We see it happen every day at our facility.

If you or your loved one is ready for treatment, please call us. We can help you determine whether or not an intervention is necessary and help you to love the addict in your life into treatment. Our intake team is available around the clock to ensure that those in need will receive help whenever they need it. We can contact your insurance provider if you are unsure whether or not addiction treatment is covered. We want you to find help for your loved one and will assist you however we can.

If you operate another treatment facility and believe in the effectiveness of our protocol, please use what you have read here to help your clients. We use our expertise to assist those who provide services to a client base that cannot afford our services. We gladly share our experience, believing strongly that all addicts should have access to the best treatment they can afford.

If you are an addict who is unable to access a treatment center that uses this protocol, use what you have learned in this book to develop the best treatment program you can in your area. It will be difficult to recover without the safety and seclusion a treatment center provides, but it can be done. You can recover.

Most addicts will never go to treatment. For those who do, Cliffside Malibu and this treatment protocol offer hope and understanding and the promise of a new and fulfilling life. Don't allow another day to pass. You deserve better. You deserve the freedom of recovery.

Resources

Following is a short list of books and websites that will provide more information on some of the major concepts presented in this book. The books listed below give more specific information regarding the ideas discussed in *Ending Addiction for Good*. The websites provide general information that informs the evidence-base of addiction treatment.

Books

Hoffer, A., & Saul A.W. (2009). *The Vitamin Cure for Alcoholism: Orthomolecular Treatment of Addictions.* Laguna Beach, CA: Basic Health Publications.

Jellinek, E. M. (1960). *The Disease Concept of Alcoholism.* New Haven, CT: College and University Press.

Kaptchuk, T. (2000). *The Web That Has No Weaver: Understanding Chinese Medicine.* New York: McGraw Hill.

Peele, S. (1989). *Diseasing of America: How We Allowed Recovery Zealots and the Treatment Industry to Convince Us We Are Out of Control.* San Francisco: Jossey-Bass.

Prochaska, J. O., J. C. Norcross, and C. C. DiClemente (2002). *Changing for Good: A Revolutionary Six-Step Program for Overcoming Bad Habits and Moving Your Life Positively Forward.* New York: Quill.

Prochaska, J. O., and J. C. Norcross (2007). *Systems of Psychotherapy: A Transtheoretical Analysis.* 6th ed. Belmont, CA: Thomson Brooks/Cole.

Siegel, D. (2010). *The Developing Mind: How Relationships and the Brain Interact to Shape Who We Are* (2nd ed.). New York: Guilford Press.

Siegel, D. (2011). *Mindsight: The New Science of Personal Transformation.* New York: Bantam Books.

Websites

Cliffside Malibu—Addiction Treatment Center
www.cliffsidemalibu.com

Dan Siegel, MD—Mindsight and Interpersonal Neurobiology
http://drdansiegel.com/home

Francine Shapiro, PhD—EMDR
http://www.emdr.com/

James Prochaska, PhD—Stages of Change and
Transtheoretical Model
http://www.prochange.com/

Marsha Linehan, PhD, ABPP—Dialectical Behavior
Therapy
http://behavioraltech.org/index.cfm

National Center for Complementary and Alternative
Medicine
http://nccam.nih.gov/health/whatiscam

National Institute on Drug Abuse
http://www.drugabuse.gov/

Psychotherapy Development Research Center
http://psychiatry.yale.edu/research/programs/clinical_
people/psychotheraphydev/index.aspx

Substance Abuse and Mental Health Services Administration
http://www.samhsa.gov/